the pregnancy & baby book

the pregnancy & baby book

Karen Evennett

PaRragon

Bath • New York • Singapore • Hong Kong • Cologne • Delhi • Melbourne

First published by Parragon in 2008

Parragon
Queen Street House
4 Queen Street
Bath BA1 1HE, UK

Copyright © Parragon Books Ltd 2008

ISBN: 978-1-4075-1902-9

Printed in China

Illustrations by Coral Mula and Melvyn Evans

Produced by the Bridgewater Book Company Ltd

The publisher would like to thank the following for permission to reproduce copyright material: Getty/Ghislain & Marie David de Lossy, p. 2; iStock, pp. 7, 8, 12, 13 (top left); Istock/Miodrag Gajic. p. 14; Istock/Amanda Rohde, p. 15, p. 55 (bottom right); Corbis/Jose L Pelaez, p. 16; Istock/Lise Gagne, p. 17; Getty, p. 13 (bottom right), p. 33; Corbis/Benelux, p. 18 (top); Istock/Michael Valdez, p. 18 (bottom); Corbis/Benjamin F Fink, p. 19 (bottom left); Istock/Nancy Kennedy, p. 19 (bottom right); Istock/Sergei Sverdelov, p. 19 (top right); Istock/Vance Smith, p. 20; Istock/Joe Klune, p. 22; Corbis/Gabe Palmer, p.25; Corbis/Simon Jarratt, p. 26; Istock/Christine Balderas, p. 27; Getty/Ruth Jenkinson, p. 30; Corbis/Sean Justice, p. 31; Getty/Zia Soleil, p. 32; Corbis/Tom Grill, p. 33; Corbis/Brooke Fasani, p. 42; Getty/Tariq Dajani, p. 43; Istock/Nathan Maxfield, p. 44; Getty/Titus, p. 46; Getty/Markus Amon, p. 47; Istock/Claude Dagenais, p. 48; Corbis/H. Schmid, p. 49; Getty/Stefanie Sudek, p. 50; Istock/Jenny Bonner, p. 52; Getty/Altrendo, p. 53; Getty/Jonathan Storey, p. 54; Getty/Caren Alpert, p. 55 (top right); Istock/David Foreman, p. 55 (bottom left); Getty/Mel Vates, p. 56; Corbis/Dann Tardif, p. 58, p. 84; Istock/Diane Diederich, p. 63 (far left); Istock/Xavier Gallego, p. 63 (centre right); Istock/Robert Dant, p. 63 (far right); Getty/Jose Luis Pelaez, p. 68; Getty/Btitt Erianson, p. 70, p. 97, p. 117; Getty/Laurence Monneret, p. 71; Istock/Al Wekelo, p. 72; Getty/Ian Hooton, p. 73, p. 82 (right), p. 85 (bottom); Getty/Christopher Bissell, p. 74; Istock/Leah-Anne Thompson, p. 75; Getty/Jonathan Nourok, p. 76; Istock/Don Bayley, p. 77; Corbis/Goupy Didier, p. 78; Istock/Tomasz Resiak, p. 79 (top); Istock/Tim Pohl, p. 79 (bottom); Getty/Michael Nischke, p. 80; Istock/Jamey Ekins, p. 81 (top), p. 92; Istock/Kenneth C Zirkel, p. 81 (bottom); Corbis/Envision, p. 82 (left); Getty/Jerome Tisne, p. 83; Getty/Dorling Kindersley, p. 85 (top); Istock/Don Bayley, p. 86; Corbis/Andersen Ross, p. 87; Getty/Andrew Olney, p. 88; Corbis, p. 89; Getty/Ellen Denuto, p. 96 (top); Istock/Mykola Velychko, p. 96 (bottom); Corbis/Rick Gomez, p. 98; Getty/Daniel Berehulak, p. 99 (top); Istock/Vivid Pixels, p. 99 (bottom); Getty/Elyse Lewin, p. 102; Getty/PM Images, p. 103; Getty/Mark Lund, p. 104; Getty/Fraser Hall, p. 105; Istock/Teresita Cortès, p. 107; Getty/Tanya Constantine, p. 108; Corbis/Michael Kller, p. 109 (top); Corbis/Cecilla Enholm, p. 109 (bottom); Corbis/Anna Peisl, p. 111; Getty/Dan Dalton, p. 112 (top); Istock/Damir Cudic, p. 112 (bottom); Getty/Michael Krasowitz, p. 113; Getty/Win Initiative, p. 114; Getty/Laureen Middley, p. 115; Getty/Victoria Snowber, p. 116; Corbis/Pinto, p. 120 (top); Corbis/Simon Smith, p 120 (bottom); Istock/Sawayasu Tsuji, p. 121; Getty/Katirnel Wittkamp, p. 122; Corbis/Bury, p. 123 (top right); Istock/Alexander Maksimenko, p. 123 (left); Istock/Anita Patterson, p. 124; Getty/Charles Gullung, p. 125 (top); Getty/Ian O'Leary, p. 125 (bottom); Corbis/S Hammid, p. 126; Getty/Dan Kenyon, p. 127 (top); Istock/Justin Horrocks, p. 127 (bottom); Getty/Stockyb, p. 128 (top); Getty/Arthur Tilley, p. 128 (bottom); Istock/Bojan Tezak, p. 129; Corbis, Brigitte Sporrer, p. 130; Getty/Ross Whitaker, p. 131; Corbis/Justyn Olby, p. 133 (top); Getty/Jen Petreshock, p. 133 (bottom); Getty/Lawrence Lawry, p. 134; Istock/Brian McEntine, p. 135; Corbis/Ariel Skelley, p. 140 (top); Getty/Jeffrey Conley, p. 140 (bottom); Getty/Ariel Skelley, p. 141 (top); Corbis/Tony Arruza, p. 141 (bottom).

Contents

Introduction

Twenty-one months is all it takes to conceive your baby and see him through to his first birthday! It is hard to think of any other time in our lives when such huge changes take place so fast. One minute you are discovering you're pregnant, and working out when you conceived and when you will give birth; the next, it seems, you are kissing your son better after his first tumble, or rejoicing in your daughter's first words. Everything can happen so quickly that, looking back, many of us wish we had taken more time to record the ups and downs that make up our child's story.

If your child one day asks, "What did you crave when you were pregnant with me?" or "When did I get my first tooth?", will you remember? This journal has space for you to record anything that seems important as you go through this journey with your new baby.

Along the way, you will find that mothers, friends, and relatives love to tell you what you should and shouldn't be doing, eating, and even feeling. All their advice will be well intentioned—if occasionally out of date—but it's important to feel confident in your own ability to manage your pregnancy and raise your baby. Becoming a mother is a very instinctive process, so trust your intuition—but do your research, too. In this book we will give you all the basic tools you need for the next 21 months. For your pregnancy, there's advice on keeping

healthy, knowing when to seek professional help, and understanding what will happen as the weeks pass and the all-important delivery approaches. For each of the three trimesters of pregnancy, there is a rundown of your growing baby's progress as well as the normal changes to your own body (together with any signs that need to be followed up with your doctor or midwife). What kind of birth do you want? Should you make a birth plan? What are the first signs of labor? What kind of pain relief should you seek? For most first-time moms, there are so many questions to ask—and we hope you will feel better informed as you go through this book.

Your pregnancy is not just about preparing to give birth— in these busy, busy months you will also be making a lot of practical plans for your baby. How should you decorate his or her room? What kind of equipment should you buy? And let's not forget names—what will you call your baby?

Once your baby arrives, do you plan to breastfeed or use a bottle? It's worth knowing that there are pros and cons to both options. For many women there will be no question—they're going to breastfeed. But what happens if that is your intention, and then, for some reason, it is not possible? It always pays to be open-minded!

Back home, how will you get your baby into a routine? How long will he sleep for? What can you do if he is a reluctant sleeper? (This is a question that troubles a huge number of new parents!)

As time goes on, how can you play with your baby to stimulate him? How can you socialize him, and what should you be feeding him and when? A baby's first year can often look like a schedule—and when you meet other new mothers they will all appear to be on top of this schedule, comparing notes about first smiles, first rolls, first solids, and first words.

You, your baby (or babies), and your pregnancy are unique, and this book is a chance to celebrate that individuality. Know what should happen and when, and record the details on our baby's milestone journal pages. It may not seem funny at the time if your baby is later than everyone else's in crawling—or if he decides not to bother at all and scoots on his bottom instead. But in years to come you will look back and laugh. We hope that a record in this journal of what happened and when will give you plenty of memories to chuckle over with your child, when you and he are old enough to see the funny side—along with those that will pull on your heart strings. We hope you'll enjoy personalizing this book as much as we've enjoyed putting it together.

Pregnancy and Care

From the earliest signs of pregnancy, you will feel different, and you will quickly start to look different, too. This is an exciting time for any woman—and her partner—but it can also be tinged with anxiety. Knowing that everything that should be happening is happening, and that you are looking after yourself and your baby as best you can, is comforting and reassuring. Use our journal pages to record your highlights, as well as any worries you may have.

Early Days

Are you pregnant, or aren't you? In the earliest days, you are the only person in the world who knows your body well enough to recognize the subtle changes that are taking place which mean you're soon to become a mother.

If you have been planning a pregnancy, you will be on red alert for any changes that indicate that your attempts have been successful. Breast tenderness and swelling, increased vaginal secretions, constipation, nausea, and fatigue can all be very early signs—or your first inkling may come from finding that the smell of coffee turns your stomach, or you have a sudden aversion to a food you normally love. Some women experience signs such as these only a week after conception—that is, around Week Three of a typical 28-day cycle.

A missed period at the beginning of the next cycle is a more definite sign—although some women experience some light bleeding ("spotting") even though they are pregnant. If you know your body well, you will quickly identify anything that's new or unusual for you.

What's your body saying?

Ƨᴥ **BREAST CHANGES** Some women experience breast pain and swelling before their period. The hormones that govern pregnancy have the same effect, though it is usually more pronounced.

Ƨᴥ **NAUSEA** Over 80 percent of pregnant women suffer from some degree of morning sickness. It's thought to be caused by chemical by-products of increased hormonal activity building up and creating general toxicity in the body. Nobody knows why some women are affected while others are not.

Ƨᴥ **FOOD AVERSIONS** Mercifully, many of us tend to go off the very things that are bad for us in pregnancy, such as coffee and alcohol, and that makes avoiding them a whole lot easier! Sometimes zinc deficiency can cause certain foods to smell or taste peculiar when you're pregnant, so make sure you're including enough zinc-rich meat or nuts in your diet. If meat smells strongly when you broil or pan-fry it, try recipes that will disguise the odor.

AM I PREGNANT?

SYMPTOM	YES	NO
Tired		
Stomach aches		
Nauseous		
Strange metallic taste in mouth		
Tender breasts		
Small bumps on nipples—Montgomery's tubercles—more prominent		
Constipated		
Needing to urinate more often		
Increased vaginal discharge		
Food aversions		

Conception to delivery

Contrary to what you may expect, your pregnancy began on the first day of your last period! It's slightly confusing, but this is how a baby's due date is estimated. So, pregnancies are expected to last 40 weeks from the date of the last period (even though conception will have actually taken place around two weeks after this date). Find the first day of your last period on the chart below, in bold type. The date immediately below it is your expected delivery date.

PREGNANCY TESTS

❧ You can do a pregnancy test on the first day of your missed period. It works by detecting the hormone human chorionic gonadotropin (hCG) in your urine. All you have to do is urinate on the end of the stick. If the hormone is present, a chemical in the stick changes color, showing the result—positive or negative—in a window. Used correctly, pregnancy tests are very accurate, though it is possible to have a false negative, when the test says you aren't pregnant but you are. If in doubt, or your period still doesn't arrive, repeat the test.

WHEN'S MY BABY DUE?

Month	1	2	3	4	5	6	7	8	9	10	11	12	13	14	15	16	17	18	19	20	21	22	23	24	25	26	27	28	29	30	31	Month
January	1	2	3	4	5	6	7	8	9	10	11	12	13	14	15	16	17	18	19	20	21	22	23	24	25	26	27	28	29	30	31	**January**
October	8	9	10	11	12	13	14	15	16	17	18	19	20	21	22	23	24	25	26	27	28	28	30	31	1	2	3	4	5	6	7	November
February	1	2	3	4	5	6	7	8	9	10	11	12	13	14	15	16	17	18	19	20	21	22	23	24	25	26	27	28				**February**
November	8	9	10	11	12	13	14	15	16	17	18	19	20	21	22	23	24	25	26	27	28	29	30	1	2	3	4	5				December
March	1	2	3	4	5	6	7	8	9	10	11	12	13	14	15	16	17	18	19	20	21	22	23	24	25	26	27	28	29	30	31	**March**
December	6	7	8	9	10	11	12	13	14	15	16	17	18	19	20	21	22	23	24	25	26	27	28	29	30	31	1	2	3	4	5	January
April	1	2	3	4	5	6	7	8	9	10	11	12	13	14	15	16	17	18	19	20	21	22	23	24	25	26	27	28	29	30		**April**
January	6	7	8	9	10	11	12	13	14	15	16	17	18	19	20	21	22	23	24	25	26	27	28	29	30	31	1	2	3	4		February
May	1	2	3	4	5	6	7	8	9	10	11	12	13	14	15	16	17	18	19	20	21	22	23	24	25	26	27	28	29	30	31	**May**
February	5	6	7	8	9	10	11	12	13	14	15	16	17	18	19	20	21	22	23	24	25	26	27	28	1	2	3	4	5	6	7	March
June	1	2	3	4	5	6	7	8	9	10	11	12	13	14	15	16	17	18	19	20	21	22	23	24	25	26	27	28	29	30		**June**
March	8	9	10	11	12	13	14	15	16	17	18	19	20	21	22	23	24	25	26	27	28	29	30	31	1	2	3	4	5	6		April
July	1	2	3	4	5	6	7	8	9	10	11	12	13	14	15	16	17	18	19	20	21	22	23	24	25	26	27	28	29	30	31	**July**
April	7	8	9	10	11	12	13	14	15	16	17	18	19	20	21	22	23	24	25	26	27	28	29	30	1	2	3	4	5	6	7	May
August	1	2	3	4	5	6	7	8	9	10	11	12	13	14	15	16	17	18	19	20	21	22	23	24	25	26	27	28	29	30	31	**August**
May	8	9	10	11	12	13	14	15	16	17	18	19	20	21	22	23	24	25	26	27	28	29	30	31	1	2	3	4	5	6	7	June
September	1	2	3	4	5	6	7	8	9	10	11	12	13	14	15	16	17	18	19	20	21	22	23	24	25	26	27	28	29	30		**September**
June	8	9	10	11	12	13	14	15	16	17	18	19	20	21	22	23	24	25	26	27	28	29	30	1	2	3	4	5	6	7		July
October	1	2	3	4	5	6	7	8	9	10	11	12	13	14	15	16	17	18	19	20	21	22	23	24	25	26	27	28	29	30	31	**October**
July	8	9	10	11	12	13	14	15	16	17	18	19	20	21	22	23	24	25	26	27	28	29	30	31	1	2	3	4	5	6	7	August
November	1	2	3	4	5	6	7	8	9	10	11	12	13	14	15	16	17	18	19	20	21	22	23	24	25	26	27	28	29	30		**November**
August	8	9	10	11	12	13	14	15	16	17	18	19	20	21	22	23	24	25	26	27	28	29	30	31	1	2	3	4	5	6		September
December	1	2	3	4	5	6	7	8	9	10	11	12	13	14	15	16	17	18	19	20	21	22	23	24	25	26	27	28	29	30	31	**December**
September	7	8	9	10	11	12	13	14	15	16	17	18	19	20	21	22	23	24	25	26	27	28	29	30	1	2	3	4	5	6	7	October

First Steps

A doctor friend described pregnancy beautifully. "Like watching a swan... On the surface there is beauty and grace, while under the water there is a frantic effort to keep everything going just right. In pregnancy, you are likely to look beautiful-'blooming'-but underneath your body is working hard to keep you and your baby in prime condition."

Your first appointment

Prenatal care exists to reassure you that everything is going smoothly-and it's a good idea to make your first appointment with your doctor or midwife as soon as you can, if only to make sure you get your allotted space on the roller coaster of appointments and prenatal classes that w follow. Don't be the mom who gets on the list for prenatal classes so late that you risk being totally unprepared if you baby happens to come early!

The list of questions and tests at your first prenatal visit may seem daunting, but for most of us it simply rules out problems, rather than raising them. In order that your doctor or midwife can build up a good picture of you and your pregnancy, be prepared to answer questions about:

- Your past and present state of health.
- Any illnesses and operations you've had.
- Any previous pregnancies or miscarriages.
- Whether there are twins in the family, or any inherited disorders.
- Your ethnic origin-because some inherited conditions are more common in certain ethnic groups.
- Your work, and that of your partner.
- Your home, and who you live with.

Ideally you will also be given a bagful of information to read and digest on the do's and don'ts of a healthy pregnancy. This is also the time to raise any early concerns and queries of your own.

You will remember for the rest of your life the moment you learned that you were pregnant.

TESTING, TESTING...

Although procedures vary from area to area, the following early prenatal tests are all to be expected:

☙ A urine test—to rule out the presence of protein, indicating infection or high blood pressure, and sugar, which may necessitate further tests to rule out diabetes.

☙ Blood pressure will be taken at the first and every subsequent prenatal visit to make sure it is within the normal range (high blood pressure can endanger both you and your baby, so it's good to know yours is where it should be).

☙ Blood is tested to establish your blood group and rule out anemia. If you're at all unsure about your rubella status, this can be checked now (rubella, or German measles, can cause cataracts, deafness, and heart lesions in your unborn baby— but most of us have had vaccinations against it as teenagers).

☙ Your weight will be taken to establish whether you are under or over the normal weight for your height, and whether this may pose any problems for you and your growing baby in the coming months.

Sharing your news can help forge new friendships and make existing relationships closer.

Telling other people

You are probably bursting to tell your friends and family that you're expecting—this is a secret that's hard to keep to yourself, your partner, and your doctor or midwife! But when is the right time to tell the rest of the world? Holding back until after the 12th week, the end of the first trimester, is fairly common practice—fueled by the fear that "something may go wrong." It's true that more than 20 percent of pregnancies (one in five) end in miscarriage—and most of them in the first 12 weeks—but, of course, the majority of pregnancies go to full term and are easy and joyous times in a new mother's life.

Telling your friends and colleagues means you can count on their support when you don't want to drink alcohol, or you're feeling too tired or nauseous to go out. This is a time when your intuition really comes into play—are you a private person, or do you like to share your emotions freely? Your parents, partner, and friends will all have an opinion about the right time to tell the world—but, ultimately, it is entirely your own decision who to tell and when.

Looking After Yourself

Tiredness is nearly always a feature of early pregnancy—it's your body's way of telling you to take it easy! Our normal need for eight hours' sleep a night shoots up in pregnancy, when ten hours' sleep (eight at night and two in the day) out of every 24 is ideal. But this can be unrealistic—especially in the earliest weeks when you are likely to be working full time, and may not even have told your boss that you are pregnant! Tiredness should be a symptom from Week Six of your pregnancy, continuing until at least Week 14 (then returning in the final few weeks before your baby is due), and it will propel you to seek sleep whenever you can. If you cannot sleep for ten hours, at least try to ensure that you get as much rest as you can—in bed, or on the sofa. It is much better to rest before you become completely exhausted and feel you cannot go on any longer.

If you find it hard to relax, book time out for yourself when an expert can help you unwind.

WHAT IF I CATCH AN INFECTION?

Some infections are more damaging than others. The riskiest to your baby are chicken pox, cytomegalovirus, fifth disease, hepatitis, Lyme disease, rubella (German measles), syphilis, listeriosis, and toxoplasmosis—but always remind your doctor that you're pregnant, even if you're contacting her about something that doesn't seem to be related to pregnancy. Certain antibiotics are considered safe in pregnancy, but any consequences of taking them will depend on how long you'd need to take them and the severity of your illness.

Listen to your body and give in to its cravings for rest—you will need much more sleep than normal.

THINGS TO AVOID

🙚 **CAT LITTER** is a source of toxoplasmosis, an infection caused by a microscopic parasite that lives in cat feces.

🙚 **SHEEP** After lambing they carry the bacteria *Chlamydia psittaci,* which can cause miscarriage.

🙚 **ALCOHOL** The latest advice is to avoid it altogether during pregnancy.

🙚 **DRUGS**—unless prescribed by a doctor who is fully aware of your stage of pregnancy.

🙚 **CIGARETTES** The nicotine constricts blood vessels in the placenta so that less oxygen and fewer nutrients reach the baby.

🙚 **JACUZZIS, HOT TUBS, AND SAUNAS** High temperatures can be hazardous and increase the risk of miscarriage—as well as dehydrating you.

🙚 **CAFFEINE** Stick to a maximum of 300 mg per day, as high levels can result in a low birth weight. A mug of coffee contains about 100 mg, a 2 oz/50 g bar of chocolate contains 50 mg.

Take good care

If you are unwell, seek medical advice before reaching for your medicine cabinet. Although only two to three percent of birth defects are caused by drugs (partly because your body fluid goes up by 14 pints, or eight liters, in pregnancy, which dilutes them), the full range of substances to which an embryo may be vulnerable is not yet known; it's therefore best to take the fewest possible medicines in pregnancy, particularly during the earliest weeks when the embryo is forming and the placenta is only just starting to be active.

Even common painkillers should be avoided because they cannot be guaranteed to be totally safe for your baby, and there are plenty of alternatives for routine problems such as headaches. Although pregnancy headaches are commonly caused by hormonal changes, they can also be triggered by fatigue (hence the need for rest), tension, stress, and hunger (don't skip meals). Give yourself a gentle facial massage to relieve headaches, or use meditation or neck exercises to relieve tension.

Happily, many women find that they are healthier than ever during pregnancy—for example, some autoimmune disorders and allergies go into remission, relieving you of the need to take drugs that you may normally rely on. Your body has a remarkable ability to protect you at this crucial time in your life—so learn to listen to it and trust it, and seek medical help when you think you may need it.

Eating for Two

Your pregnancy is not the time to start a diet, in the weight-loss sense—but it may be an opportunity to improve the one you have. Recent studies suggest that pregnant women who eat a lot of junk food—fries, chips, donuts, etc.—are more likely to give birth to children who crave this kind of food and will struggle to maintain an ideal weight. So the best way to interpret the old saying that you're "eating for two" when you're pregnant is that you have two lives to consider. You do not need to double your calorie intake to do this

(2,500 is ideal—just 400 more than usual), but you do have to remember that your baby is relying on what you eat and drink to get adequate nourishment in the uterus.

A well-balanced diet should contain something from all the food groups—dairy, fruit, vegetables, meat, eggs, fish, and carbohydrates—and, while you're pregnant, you should endeavor to include something from each of these groups every day. Do stick to fresh foods. For more information about healthy eating, see our list of foods to aim for.

Aim to eat a rainbow of fresh fruits and vegetables to pump variety into your diet.

...come a milk drinker again—or choose yogurt or cheese if
...u prefer it.

Aim for:

FOUR SERVINGS OF PROTEIN—meat, fish, eggs,
...eese, legumes—daily. Protein is composed of amino acids,
...e building blocks of human cells, and research has shown
...at inadequate protein consumption during pregnancy can
...esult in a smaller than average baby.

...xamples: 3 x 8 fl oz/225 ml glasses of skim milk; two large
...ggs plus two egg whites; 3 oz/85 g red meat; 2½ oz/70 g
...hicken; 3 oz/85 g cheese; 3½ oz/100g fish.

TWO SERVINGS OF VITAMIN C This is needed
...y both you and your baby for a multitude of nutrient-
...tilizing processes.

...xamples: 2 small oranges; ½ glass of orange juice; ½ cup
...trawberries; 1½ large tomatoes; ½ mango; ½ small red or
...reen pepper.

FOUR SERVINGS OF CALCIUM FOODS These are
...eeded for muscle, heart, and nerve development.

...xamples of calcium portions: 8 fl oz/225 ml glass of skim
...ilk; 1½ oz/40 g cheddar cheese; 10 dried figs; 4 oz/115 g
...anned salmon with bones.

**THREE SERVINGS OF GREEN LEAFY VEGETABLES
...OR YELLOW FRUIT AND VEGETABLES**—for betacarotene,
...vital for cell growth.

...Examples: slice of cantaloupe melon; two large apricots;
½ mango; fistful of broccoli, spinach, or kale.

**TWO OR MORE SERVINGS OF OTHER FRUIT AND
VEGETABLES**—for fiber, vitamins, and minerals.

FIVE SERVINGS OF WHOLE GRAINS AND BEANS—
for B vitamins, needed for healthy baby development.

Examples: 1 slice whole-grain bread; fistful of cooked brown
rice; fistful of baked beans or chickpeas.

Also try to include some iron-rich foods (e.g. beef, pumpkin,
spinach, dried fruits) every day for your baby's developing
blood supply as well as your own, which is expanding.

MORNING SICKNESS

**If you can't stomach the thought of all this healthy
food because you are suffering with morning sickness,
you're not alone—over 80 percent of pregnant women
suffer from morning sickness in some way. Nobody
knows why it happens or why some women are
affected while others are not, but you're more likely to
suffer if you also get motion sick. In fact, the solutions
that work for motion sickness can also work best for
morning sickness—sucking something with ginger in
it (ginger helps food pass more rapidly through the
digestive system and also reduces stimulation to the
part of the brain that prompts nausea), or wearing a
pressure point motion sickness wristband.**

IT ALSO HELPS TO:

Get as much rest as possible.

Separate drinks from meals.

Steer clear of fried foods and caffeine.

Avoid cooking as much as possible. (Show
this page to your partner!)

Foods to Avoid

While there are plenty of foods you may wish to avoid–just because they don't appeal to you, or taste stronger than usual right now–there are some that really must be avoided, or treated with caution:

Food hazards

🐦 **UNPASTEURIZED MILK AND CHEESE** can contain the bacteria listeria which, although causing only flulike symptoms in an adult, can lead to miscarriage in early pregnancy or premature labor and the risk of stillbirth mid-pregnancy. Listeriosis is extremely rare, affecting only one pregnancy in every 20,000, and the infection can be treated with antibiotics–however, it is better to avoid this risk in the first place. Stick to hard cheeses such as Cheddar, Edam, and Parmesan. Mozzarella, feta, marscapone and processed cream cheeses, cottage cheese, and spreads are also OK, but avoid the soft mold-ripened ones like Brie and Camembert, along with blue-veined cheeses such as blue cheese, and goat cheese (Chèvre).

The restaurant cheeseboard can become hazardous in pregnancy.

🐦 **BAGGED SALADS** should be re-washed after opening even if they come "ready to serve," as they may carry the same toxoplasma parasite that's found in cat litter and which can cause miscarriage and birth defects, including brain damage. They may also carry listeria or salmonella.

🐦 **UNDERCOOKED MEAT** is another possible source of toxoplasma, so make sure it is cooked right through (you should forego rare beef and lamb for the next few months).

🐦 **RUNNY EGG YOLK** runs the risk of carrying the salmonella bug, and should be avoided "just in case." Salmonella can cause serious vomiting, diarrhea, fever, and dehydration, and although it's very unlikely your baby will be harmed, it's best to avoid the risk.

Salad produce should be washed before eating to remove bacteria.

oking kills salmonella, so make sure you cook an egg until s solid. For a boiled egg, that's about seven minutes. Fried gs should be fried on both sides, and, if you're poaching, so for five minutes.

🐟 **MAYONNAISE**, unless it's the store-bought variety hich is usually pasteurized and therefore safe), is made ing raw eggs and should be avoided. Most prepacked ndwiches containing mayonnaise will use the type that's fe—but, if in doubt, check it out!

🐟 **FISH** is a good source of protein to include in your egnancy diet, and you should aim for at least two servings week (including one portion of oily fish such as fresh tuna, ackerel, salmon, sardines, trout, and kipper). However, ark, swordfish, and marlin should be avoided because they ontain high levels of pollutants such as mercury, which can arm your baby's nervous system. Basically, the higher up e food chain a fish is, the more toxic it will be. Tuna has e potential to be affected by the same pollutants, though a lesser degree, and consumption should be limited to no ore than two steaks (weighing 5 oz/140 g cooked), or two edium-sized cans of tuna a week.

🐟 **LIVER** and liver products such as pâté should be voided while you're pregnant, as they contain very high

Preparing your own fruit and vegetables may be time-consuming but it's the healthiest option.

levels of vitamin A, which has been shown to cause birth defects. Pâté can also be a carrier of listeria.

🐟 **SUSHI** is fine to eat as long as any raw fish in it has been frozen beforehand. This may sound strange, but fish can sometimes contain tiny worms that could make you ill— and the freezing process kills them. Most store-bought sushi is safe, as it has to contain fish that has been frozen for at least 24 hours. But if you're in doubt, avoid it altogether.

Make sure you know where your sushi came from before eating it.

Check with your doctor before taking any vitamin supplements in pregnancy.

Keeping Fit

Your grandmother may have been warned not to take exercise in pregnancy, but these days it is generally considered a benefit. Regular exercise helps your circulation, builds stamina for the birth, and makes it much easier to get back into shape afterward. However, this is not the time to start training to run a marathon, and if you've been used to doing fairly strenuous sports, you must adapt to a gentler routine. If you're not physically active, only take up something easy such as swimming or walking—just 30-60 minutes a day is all you need to do. If you are feeling fit and healthy, it can be difficult to remember that you are in a more fragile state than usual, but if you've always been very athletic, remember that pregnancy softens your joints and ligaments, making you much more susceptible to straining yourself if you overdo it.

If you attend a mainstream exercise class, let your teacher know that you're pregnant.

Staying active

❧ **AEROBICS** Stick to a low-impact class and don't jump up and down or allow yourself to become overheated. Drink plenty of water before and after classes, and limit yourself to 30 minutes.

❧ **SQUASH** Overstretching and pulling muscles and ligaments is a risk—and you should not jump up and down.

❧ **CYCLING** As long as you don't fall off, this is safe exercise; but remember that as you get bigger you will have more weight at the front, which could cause you to lose your balance.

❧ **GOLF** Walking the average 9-hole course (2½ miles/ 4 km) is good exercise, taken at a gentle pace, but be careful not to twist your knees and pelvis too much.

Swimming is a safe and supportive exercise for your growing bump and will keep you fit during pregnancy.

PELVIC FLOOR EXERCISES

🐋 If "pelvic floor" sounds like a close cousin of linoleum, welcome to the new world of motherhood–in which you will be introduced to this hitherto unnoticed part of your body for the first time. The pelvic floor is the sling of muscles that helps hold the pelvic organs in place, and pelvic floor exercises will be important for the remainder of your life. Without them, these muscles can become slack, making sexual intercourse less enjoyable and putting you at risk of stress incontinence. In pregnancy the increase of the hormone progesterone softens tissues, making them more stretchy. As the pelvic floor also softens, and is under additional pressure from the weight of your growing baby, this is a good time to start strengthening it.

Lie down with your knees bent up and your feet on the floor. Tighten your vagina, urethra, and anus together. Now think of the three tightened areas as a drawbridge, and try to lift it up inside you. Hold, breathing slowly in and out, then slowly let it down in as many stages as you can manage. Once you have mastered this exercise, you will be able to do it anywhere–even when you are standing in line at the supermarket–and nobody will know what you are doing.

A strong pelvic floor is essential, even if you're planning to have a Cesarean.

🐋 SWIMMING is a wonderful exercise in pregnancy, as your body weight is supported by the water.

🐋 JOGGING If you're already a jogger, carry on, but take some advice from a gym instructor or physiotherapist on adapting your stride to avoid jarring.

🐋 TENNIS is OK for the first trimester, but after that stick to practicing shots rather than running around.

🐋 SKIING The safest time to ski is in your second trimester (12-24 weeks)–but try not to fall heavily and avoid high speeds and crowded trails. In late pregnancy skiing

becomes physically difficult and potentially dangerous, because it could induce a premature labor.

🐋 HORSEBACK RIDING It's recommended that you avoid activities with the risk of hard falls, so, no matter how much of a pro you are, riding is out during pregnancy.

🐋 WALKING is a great low-impact aerobic exercise. Even if you hate all other forms of exercise, try to take a 30-60 minute walk every day. As well as keeping you fit, walking is amazingly uplifting and energizing, good for your mind as well as your body.

Yoga for Pregnancy

Apart from the fact that it is extremely relaxing, helping you switch off from stress and winding your body down for the sleep you need in pregnancy (and which can sometimes be frustratingly elusive), yoga is an excellent way to maintain your suppleness and prepare for the birth. It's also a great way of meeting other moms-to-be if you attend a class aimed specifically at pregnant women. If you already attend a mainstream yoga class, and want to continue, it's important to let your instructor know that you are pregnant so she can adapt certain postures to suit you.

Postures for pregnancy

Even if you have never done yoga before, there are some easy postures that will be very beneficial during pregnancy.

CORPSE

Great for early pregnancy, this deeply relaxing posture, as its name suggests, involves lying on your back on the floor. Keep your body in a nice straight line, arms by your sides (palms facing up), legs rolling out loosely from the hips, and your feet falling gently out to the side. Use this posture to practice deep breathing, breathing in and out to the count of four, then, if this is comfortable, to the count of six, and finally eight, then back down to six, and four.

As you breathe in, feel your diaphragm move downward. As you breathe out, it will relax upward. This gentle exercise

Yoga is a contemplative exercise regime that is good for the mind as well as the body.

is designed to make more room in the abdomen and will make later pregnancy more comfortable. After 30 weeks of pregnancy, however, the weight of the baby can press uncomfortably on nerves and blood vessels, causing pain or dizziness. From this time on, instead of lying flat on your back (even in bed), it is better to lie on your side, with a cushion or pillow between your knees.

The Corpse is ideal for practicing deep breathing and will make more room in the abdomen.

UPTURNED BEETLE

Some women are so tense that when they do start to let go, through yoga breathing, they can feel quite light-headed. If this happens to you, try this posture—but only up to your 30th week, as it involves lying on your back.

Lie on your back with your spine extended and chin tucked in. Bend your knees and place one hand on each knee. Feel your spine in contact with the floor, and press your tailbone, waist, and neck toward the floor. Now, gently holding your knees, rotate them in small circles with your hands, softening your hips and lower back. This is a very relaxing position, ideal for early pregnancy (up to 14 weeks). Just watch the natural rhythm of your breath, until you feel ready to sit up again.

Lying like an upturned beetle will stop you feeling light-headed and is an ideal position for early pregnancy.

This deeply relaxing position helps you breathe more easily, stretches your back, and relieves aching legs.

LEGS UP THE WALL

This posture is also deeply relaxing, but again unsuitable after 30 weeks. Start by sitting side on to a wall. Lie down and swivel on your bottom until your legs are up the wall, with no space between your buttocks and the wall, and your back is in a neat right angle to your legs. Have a cushion under your head, if it's more comfortable, and place your hands under the tip of the back of your head (not under your neck). The position opens your chest (enabling easier breathing), relaxes tired legs, and stretches out your back. If you like, you can let your legs fall gently to the side. To get out of the posture, swivel yourself side on to the wall again as you bring your legs back down.

🐚 Only hold a posture for as long as it is comfortable—this may be just a minute or so to start with.

Weeks 1-12: Your Growing Baby

Much of what will make your baby the person he or she is going to become is determined by the very first day of your pregnancy. At the point of conception, the sperm and egg fuse to create a single cell, called the zygote, which contains the genetic information that will decide your baby's gender, hair, and eye color, and even aspects of his or her personality and intelligence. Even vulnerability to certain diseases and any special talents are predetermined on this crucial first day.

🐦 Four weeks later, eyes and ears are starting to form, and the baby's head and "tail" are present.

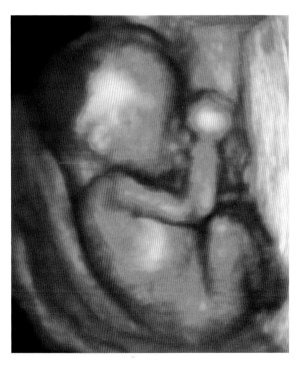

A 3D-ultrasound scan—a recent development not yet widely available—gives a remarkably detailed image of your growing baby.

🐦 By six to eight weeks, the baby is the size of a kidney bean, facial features are forming, and bones are developing. The spinal canal has closed around the spinal cord, helped by the presence of folic acid in your diet—the reason we are now told to take this important mineral before and after conception is to reduce the risk of neural tube defects such as spina bifida.

🐦 The heartbeat can be detected by Week 10. At this stage, with the heart already fully formed, the embryo is called a fetus and has a human appearance—with eyes, eyelids, and ears.

🐦 By 12 weeks, the end of your first trimester, the fetus can produce urine and his or her gender can be identified. Your baby even has 32 permanent tooth buds already!

The ultrasound scan

Ultrasound scanning has been widely used for nearly 40 years. The test gives a two- or three-dimensional picture of the developing baby, using high-frequency sound waves.

You will probably be offered a survey ultrasound around 17-20 weeks, to detect any abnormalities. The ultrasound procedure is completely painless. A device called a transducer is placed on the abdomen, issuing sound waves which bounce off the baby's tissues to be translated into a rough picture of your baby. The main advantage of the scan is that it reassures you that your baby is has a healthy heartbeat and is the age you have already calculated. And if you want to know whether you should be debating girl or boy names, you can usually find out your baby's gender during this ultrasound.

PRENATAL TESTS

Toward the end of the first trimester, you may be offered first trimester screening, which combines results from three tests to screen for genetic disorders such as Down's syndrome.

The AFP (alphafetoprotein) test, from 11 weeks, is a blood test that measures the AFP protein made by all unborn babies. Low levels can mean that the baby has an increased risk of Down's syndrome, while high levels may indicate a risk of spina bifida.

Down's syndrome is the largest single cause of learning difficulties, and comes with a range of health problems, too. The majority of these are of the niggling variety—runny noses, earaches, and sticky eyes (all treatable)—although up to one in five children may have what is known as an AV canal defect of the heart, which can wreak havoc with circulation. That said, most people with Down's syndrome now live long and happy lives, many living healthily right through to their seventies.

The nuchal translucency scan, at 11-14 weeks, harmlessly measures the fold of skin behind the baby's neck, which, combined with your age, is used to estimate the likelihood of Down's syndrome. It is often combined with blood tests to optimize the chance of an accurate result, and, as such, identifies the largest number of Down's babies.

CVS (chorionic villus sampling), from 11 weeks, involves a needle being passed through your abdomen, under ultrasound guidance, and a tiny sample of the placenta being taken for analysis. There is a one percent risk of miscarriage from CVS.

Weeks 1-12: Your Body

You are likely to become very body conscious in this first trimester—and rightly so. Your waistline is expanding (particularly noticeable if you're very slim and have little excess flesh for your growing bump to hide behind), and numerous other changes serve as constant reminders that you are now pregnant.

If morning sickness is not a problem for you, your appetite is likely to increase—don't fight it, but do eat sensibly! Some weight gain is normal in the first trimester, but not obligatory, and it is possible to put on too much weight too soon. If you've gained more than 3 lb/1.7 kg by the second month, look at your diet and cut out items such as fries, chips, cakes, and candies. Cravings may make this seem impossible—you often crave the very goodies you're supposed to be avoiding—but a balanced diet, with plenty of whole grains and pulses, can help with this.

Dealing with digestion

An altogether different stomach problem, common in the first trimester, is constipation. Elimination is more sluggish now that the muscles around the bowel are beginning to relax, and the pressure from your growing womb also inhibit normal bowel activity. Making sure you get plenty of fruit and vegetables, washed down with the recommended 8-10 glasses of water every day, will help to maintain the digestiv process and keep constipation at bay—as will a walk or swim

As hormones are relaxing the gastro-intestinal tract, another problem that can arise is indigestion, which can cause you to bloat and look much more pregnant than you really are. Although unpleasant for you, you can be reassured that the slowing down of your digestive processe allows better absorption of nutrients into your bloodstream and to the placenta, which feeds your baby.

Celebrate your changing body, but remember to eat sensibly so that you don't put on too much weight.

AVOIDING HEARTBURN AND INDIGESTION

🐦 Wear loose clothing so your stomach isn't squeezed.

🐦 Eat six small meals a day rather than three large ones.

🐦 Eat slowly, taking small mouthfuls, and chew thoroughly.

🐦 Avoid fried and fatty foods and carbonated drinks.

🐦 Sleep with your head supported on an extra pillow.

🐦 Bend at the knees instead of the waist—a good habit anyway, now you're pregnant.

WHY CAN'T I SLEEP?

It's one of the frustrating ironies of early pregnancy that, despite increased fatigue during the day, you cannot get to sleep at night! If this applies to you, try the following:

🐾 Eat early in the evening so you don't go to bed feeling full, but if you're hungry before bedtime have a sleep-inducing snack such as a banana so hunger pangs don't keep you awake.

🐾 Develop a bedtime routine with a slow pace after dinner, and a relaxing bath before bed. Try to go to bed at the same time every night.

🐾 Don't take work to bed with you—it will make your mind race and prevent you from sleeping.

🐾 Make sure your diet contains enough iron-rich foods. Iron deficiency can make it harder to get to sleep.

🐾 Avoid caffeine, which is a classic culprit for a restless night.

Bananas are a good source of tryptophan, which helps you get to sleep.

Your emotions

Irritability, irrationality, weepiness, and moodiness are normal in pregnant women, especially in the very early stages and if you normally suffer with PMS. Some ambivalence about the pregnancy is also quite usual—strange as it may seem when the baby has been planned and longed for. The usual rules—eating sensibly, exercising regularly, and getting enough rest—apply to mood swings too, and should help to keep your feelings in perspective. But see your doctor if you're finding it hard to cope. It's important to take all the help available now, so you have the strength of mind to care for yourself and your growing baby.

HOW YOUR BABY GROWS

6 weeks

12 weeks

My First Trimester

My feelings

....
....
....
....
....

How I look

....
....
....
....
....

Important dates

....
....
....
....
....

My First Trimester

Things to ask my doctor

....

....

....

....

....

....

....

I'm happy about

....

....

....

....

....

....

I'm worried about

....

....

....

....

....

Weeks 13-28: Your Growing Baby

Your baby starts this trimester the size of your fist, but in the first four weeks she will grow more than at any other time in the womb—reaching 5½ inches/14 cm and weighing around 7 oz/200 g. She's already very active (although you won't be able to feel her just yet), her nervous system is up and running, and she can suck her thumb and swallow. She can hear sounds echoing through your amniotic fluid, and reacts to them. Her heartbeat should be strong, and it's twice as fast as yours!

She's growing so rapidly that her head and body are now in better proportion and she doesn't look so top-heavy. As the trimester progresses, her face looks more human and her hair, eyebrows, and eyelashes are all beginning to grow, along with her fingernails and toenails. If you could see

You will love feeling the baby move (known as the quickening when it first happens)—and your baby will get to know your touch, too.

EARLY SECOND TRIMESTER

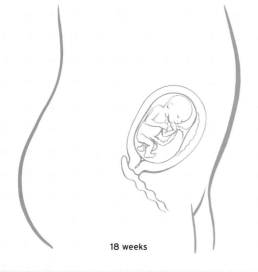

18 weeks

into the womb, she would be red and wrinkly and her bones and blood vessels would be visible because she doesn't yet have a layer of fat under her skin to hide them. Her eyes are closed until the 26th week, but REM sleep, associated with dreaming, is beginning. In fact, from Week 20 the baby has her own cycle of waking and sleeping, which doesn't necessarily correspond with yours. Your baby can already strum the umbilical cord—and if she gets the hiccups you will definitely know about it!

Between 25 and 28 weeks her body gets stronger, and the brain is developing well, too. By the end of the trimester she is about 10 inches/26.5 cm long, and weighs about 3 lb/1.3 kg. It's comforting to know that from now on your baby will have a good chance of survival if born prematurely.

FIRST KICKS

🐦 Feeling your baby move for the first time normally happens around Week 16 or 17, and if you've had a baby before you will recognize those flutters earlier and know that they're coming from your baby, not your stomach! Conversely, if you are quite well padded you may have to wait for more vigorous movements, later on, before they register on your inner Richter scale. Early on it can feel like a butterfly fluttering inside you; later it will feel like squirming, rolling, and kicking!

The best time to tune into your baby's movements is if you lie down quietly after an evening snack or meal. If there ever comes a point when you are concerned—maybe because your baby was previously very active, but has now been static for 24 hours—call your doctor or midwife immediately.

The ultrasound scan is one of the most exciting events for every expectant parent in the pregnancy diary.

LATE SECOND TRIMESTER

24 weeks

Tests in this trimester

As well as the very exciting ultrasound scan at 18-20 weeks, when you will see your baby for the first time and hear her heartbeat loud and clear, there will be a number of other screening tests on offer from Week 16, again mostly with the aim of identifying or ruling out Down's syndrome. Ask your midwife or doctor about the range of tests available, but typical tests include blood tests such as the AFP4 or Quad screen (which checks for AFP along with two hormones, estriol and human chorionic gonadotropin) and a serum test which additionally checks for levels of a substance called inhibin A.

Amniocentesis accurately detects Down's and a few other chromosomal abnormalities (but not the full range, which runs to over 400). It can also detect the baby's gender but is not used for this unless there's a risk that the gender of the baby could predict a problem such as muscular dystrophy. The main risk of amniocentesis, which involves drawing fluid from around the baby using a syringe, is that it can cause trauma to the baby, placenta, or umbilical cord, and there is a small risk (0.5-3 percent) of miscarriage as a result.

Weeks 13-28: Your Body

The great news about the second trimester is that this is the time women famously gain an energy boost—so make the most of it, you may finally be feeling that you are beginning to "bloom!" Many women wait until now to tell friends and relatives about the pregnancy, and it may be only now—when you've seen your baby's heart on the ultrasound and can see your bulge emerging—that the reality sinks in for you, too. You're likely to become clumsier now, due to a combination of factors: loosening joints, water retention, and lack of concentration, all of which are part of being pregnant. Your poor concentration (it's because of your hormones!) can also make you forgetful and you can feel as if you're shedding brain cells. Recognizing that it's normal should help you through what is, after all, a temporary phase. But minimize the disruption to your life and reduce stress by getting into the habit of writing yourself To Do lists, and ticking off the tasks as you complete them.

Other things you may notice

🦢 **SKIN CHANGES**, caused by the pregnancy hormones, include a darkening complexion known as chloasma, or "the mask of pregnancy"; a dark line down your tummy (linea nigra) and hyperpigmentation (darkening of the skin) in high-friction areas like between the thighs. Heat rash is more likely, due to increased eccrine perspiration (the type that covers the whole body), but the good news is that you will have less body odor as apocrine perspiration—the kind produced by glands under your arms and in the genital area—lessens in pregnancy.

🦢 **BACKACHE** is a side effect of your joints loosening and it will be exacerbated by poor posture. A good way to hold your body correctly, when standing, is to imagine you have a bowl of water on each hip and you mustn't spill it.

Tune into what's normal for you and your body, and try not to feel pressured by friends' experiences.

Sitting at a desk, make sure your work surface is at the correct height so you don't have to slump forward. You should be able to sit with your feet on the floor, a little apart, and your knees should be lower than your hips. A wedge cushion on your chair can push your spine into the correct position so you don't sink into your pelvis.

🦢 **LOWER ABDOMINAL PAIN**, caused by the stretching of the muscles and ligaments supporting the uterus, is normal and may be sharp or cramplike—especially when you stand up after sitting or lying, or when you cough. Do mention it to your midwife, but don't worry too much.

rsistent upper abdominal pain, just under your ribs, could dicate pre-eclampsia, which is very dangerous to both you d your baby—so this should be reported immediately.

◄ **LEG CRAMPS** can propel you out of bed in the iddle of the night and are thought to be caused by cess phosphorus and too little calcium in the blood, nich may mean cutting down on meat and milk (sources phosphorus) and finding other ways of getting your lcium—for example, from almonds. Discuss the problem, id any dietary changes, with your doctor or midwife. If ou do suffer cramping, try to straighten your leg and then owly flex your toes and ankle toward your nose. If you an't get rid of the pain, see your doctor. Continuous pain the calf may be a sign of a blood clot, which needs urgent edical treatment.

HOW MUCH WEIGHT SHOULD I GAIN?

◄ Normal weight gain in pregnancy is 25–35 lb/11.3–16 kg, which includes the weight of the baby, placenta, amniotic fluid, and your own body changes. If you started the pregnancy underweight, expect to gain 35 lb/16 kg or more. If you're overweight, try to gain less than 25 lbs/11.3 kg.

For many women, being pregnant brings new body confidence as well as the classic glow.

My Second Trimester

How I'm feeling

....

....

....

The first time I felt my baby kick

....

....

....

The baby stuff we're discussing

....

....

....

Important dates

....

....

....

....

My Second Trimester

Things to ask my doctor

I'm happy about

I'm worried about

Weeks 29-40: Your Growing Baby

The last trimester often feels like the longest—it's like the final leg of a journey to a new destination. You're probably excited, apprehensive, and finding it hard to imagine your arrival—or, in this case, your baby's!

By the start of this third trimester, your baby is fully formed but growing bigger and stronger, ready for birth. At 30 weeks the average baby is about 16 inches/40 cm from head to bottom, and by 32 weeks, she's likely to be lying head downward, ready for birth. She's still growing rapidly, gaining around 10 oz/280 g a week. Her lungs are secreting surfactant, which keeps them expanded, ready to breathe when she's born. Her head is growing faster than the rest of her, to accommodate her growing brain, and her skin, which was quite wrinkled before, is now smoother. Both the verni (a protective waxy coating) and lanugo (soft downy hair) a beginning to disappear.

The baby's activity is changing, too, becoming more organized and consistent, with clearly defined periods of rest and activity.

Your baby's presentation

Crucially, toward the end of the third trimester your midwif will have worked out your baby's "presentation"—in other words, which part of her is facing the womb's exit. There ar several possibilities:

❧ **CEPHALIC**—the most common presentation position— means that your baby is head down, with the top of the head (the vertex) pointing toward your cervix, and the chin tucked into the chest. This is the best position for delivery, because the narrowest part of the head comes out first and the baby's head is protected. Cephalic presentation can be described in one of six ways—left occipito-anterior, right occipito-anterior, left occipito-lateral, right occipito-lateral, left occipito-posterior, or right occipito-posterior—describing where the baby's head is when descending the birth canal.

❧ **ANTERIOR** means the baby's back is facing out, lying inside the curve of your abdomen.

❧ **BREECH** means the baby is lying bottom-down rather than head-down at full term. This usually means an automatic Cesarean section, but many mothers do now successfully deliver vaginally.

❧ **BROW** means that although the baby is head down, the neck is extended so that the brow or face is pointing to

EARLY THIRD TRIMESTER

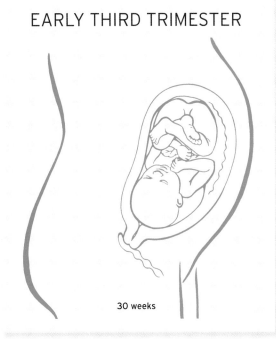

30 weeks

POSITIONS FOR BIRTH

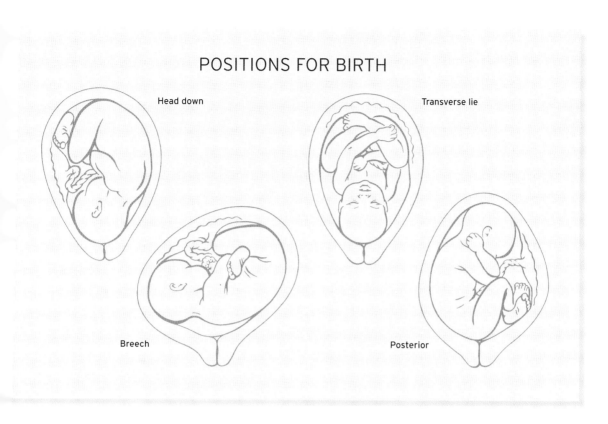

Head down

Transverse lie

Breech

Posterior

e cervix. Delivered in this position, the baby may suffer
ome facial bruising, but this will quickly disappear.

🐦 **FACE** means the face is toward the cervix. It can make
elivery awkward and stressful for the baby. Her neck can be
exed back in the process, and you may want to take her to
cranial osteopath in the early weeks of life.

🐦 **OCCIPITO-ANTERIOR OR POSTERIOR** means the
ack of your baby's head is facing the front (anterior) or
ack (posterior) of your pelvis as it descends the birth canal.
the baby remains in an occipito-posterior position, the labor
ay be slower and more painful (known as "back labor").

🐦 **TRANSVERSE LIE** means the baby is lying across the
omb rather than head down. If this remains the case at the
tart of labor, a Cesarean section is unavoidable.

🐦 **UNSTABLE LIE** means the baby keeps changing
osition between prenatal visits after 36 weeks. This could
lso result in a Cesarean section if your baby doesn't
tabilize in early labor.

LATE THIRD TRIMESTER

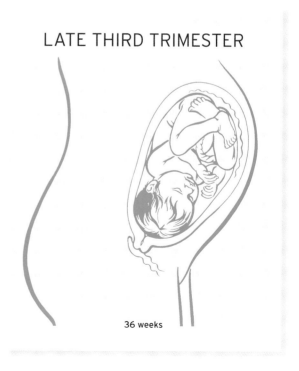

36 weeks

This is both an emotional and a body-conscious time, and you may be jumpy about any little sign that could indicate an early labor. As ever, take a serious note of any abdominal pain, and mention it to your midwife or doctor. Lower abdominal pain may be a symptom of your ligaments stretching, but if the pain is continuous or very uncomfortable, your midwife will be able to advise you on the best ways to support your bump.

You may have been experiencing practice contractions—known as Braxton Hicks contractions—for many weeks, but these can be quite strong in the third trimester. As your baby's due date approaches, they may be especially frequent, intense, and painful. To relieve any discomfort, change position—get up and walk around, or lie down.

Only weeks to go until you meet your baby for the first time—you may already be able to identify her limbs, head, and bottom!

Rest and relaxation

Coping with pain and carrying so much extra weight can b draining, and adds to your fatigue, which increases again this trimester. It can be exacerbated by your bulk preventi you from sleeping properly, and any worries about the bir that are keeping your mind ticking over. As always, though fatigue is a sign that you should look after yourself. Rest and relax as much as you can, and save your strength for your delivery. If you feel no better after resting, report this to your doctor at your next checkup.

Another problem that can interfere with your sleep is heat—your body is naturally warmer during pregnancy, but it is important to take steps to prevent yourself from overheating. At night, switch to a lighter-weight duvet if you're getting too hot. By day, dress sensibly in layers of

STRETCH MARKS

Whether you get stretch marks in pregnancy depends on whether you have an inherited tendency toward them. The stretch occurs in the collagen level of the skin and is thought to be linked to production of corticosteroids in pregnancy. The marks may appear on your abdomen, thighs, breasts, and buttocks, and, although quite alarmingly reddish purple to begin with, they usually fade within six months of delivery. Regular exercise (especially walking and swimming) will improve your circulation and help keep them under control, and a daily massage with wheatgerm oil scented with a drop of lavender oil will keep your skin supple and may reduce the marks.

...tton clothing that allow your skin to breathe—and, as ever, ...member to drink plenty of water!

Swelling

...me degree of swelling in the feet, ankles, and lower legs ...considered completely normal in pregnancy—75 percent ...us experience it, especially toward the end of the day, ...hot weather, or if we've been standing for a long time. ...sually it disappears overnight. Drinking plenty of water ...elps prevent water retention, but spread it through the day. ...your swelling (edema) is causing you discomfort, put your ...gs up, wear comfortable shoes, and avoid elastic-top socks ... stockings. Support tights also help, but put them on first ...ning in the morning, before the swelling has started.

Although we have just pointed out that some degree ...f swelling is completely normal, please note that we are ...alking only about swelling of the feet, ankles, and lower ...egs. It is not normal for the face or hands to become ...wollen or puffy, and if you notice this you must notify ...our doctor or midwife immediately as this could be ...sign of pre-eclampsia, which is a life-threatening (and ...ery common) condition that needs speedy treatment.

AROMATHERAPY

Essential oils can help with a number of problems in the third trimester—including facilitating sleep and relaxation and helping to prepare your body for labor. However, make sure you take expert advice before embarking on your own aromatherapy regime. A number of oils are considered a danger in pregnancy—and some experts recommend using no essential oils in the first trimester. The safest oils for use in pregnancy are geranium, mandarin, neroli, ylang-ylang, grapefruit, lavender, cypress, ginger, black pepper, coriander, sandalwood, pine, rose otto, and patchouli.

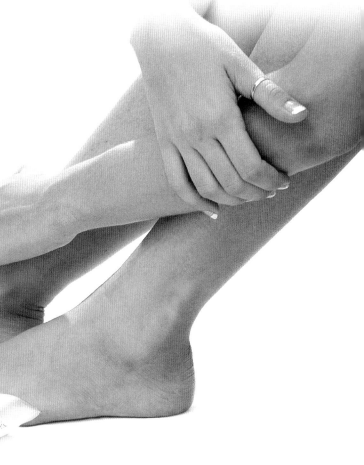

A pedicure can make you feel like a woman again, and not just a mom-to-be.

My Third Trimester

My typical day

My Third Trimester

Tips I've discovered

Dates to remember

Common Worries

It is natural to be apprehensive during pregnancy—you have a big responsibility on your hands, and you don't want to do anything that could jeopardize your baby's health.

Things to consider

MEDICINES As discussed earlier in this chapter (see page 15), it is important to talk to your midwife or doctor about any medicines you are taking, and not to reach for your usual over-the-counter remedies before checking that they are safe. This applies to herbal medicines and essential oils as much as to proprietary drugs.

TRAVEL Although there's no medical reason why you can't fly when you are pregnant, your risk of deep-vein thrombosis is slightly increased (to help avoid this, keep hydrated and do ankle rotations to increase blood flow). The majority of airlines won't allow you to fly from 32 weeks, and you will find it difficult to get travel insurance at this stage of pregnancy.

SEX Most couples find that their sexual relationship changes in pregnancy for better or worse, but, in a normal low-risk pregnancy, it is safe to continue having sex, even close to your baby's due date.

DIZZINESS AND FAINTING Dizziness in the first trimester may be related to the pressure on your blood supply to meet your rapidly expanding circulatory system, and you can also feel dizzy if your blood sugar is low because you've gone too long without food. However, if you get a lot of dizziness in pregnancy, mention it to your doctor and always report any actual fainting promptly.

HEAVY LIFTING If you have a job that involves a lot of heavy lifting and physical work, let your boss know as soon as possible that you are pregnant so you can be transferred to less strenuous duties. Even if you feel that you can continue as normal, there's a slightly increased risk of miscarriage or premature labor if you lift heavy objects and it's not worth the risk.

HAIR DYE Although there's no research linking the chemicals in hair dye to pregnancy problems, you may be trying to avoid chemicals anyway—in which case a natural dye such as henna may work as an alternative.

IN GOOD HANDS

If you know your body well, and report any worries to your health carer, you are doing all you can to assure a healthy pregnancy and baby. Routine blood pressure and urine checks will enable your midwife to monitor your risk of conditions such as hypertension, pre-eclampsia, and gestational diabetes. Keep all your prenatal appointments and report any concerns you may have.

Discuss worries with your doctor or midwife, and don't be embarrassed about taking up their time—that's what they're there for.

WHEN YOU MUST WORRY

It's always a good idea to be body-aware and to know what's normal for you and what's not; but this is particularly the case in pregnancy, so report any concerns to your doctor or midwife. Some symptoms (even those that may seem irrelevant) are warning signs that must be taken extremely seriously. They include the following:

🐚 Vaginal bleeding could be a sign of miscarriage.

🐚 Severe morning sickness–a condition known as hyperemesis gravidarum, in which you can keep nothing down–may require you to be hospitalized for treatment.

🐚 Very itchy limbs could indicate the liver condition Cholestasis of Pregnancy, which, left untreated, can lead to stillbirth.

🐚 Flulike symptoms could be caused by an infection harmful to your baby.

🐚 Leg pain could be a sign of deep-vein thrombosis.

🐚 Severe headache could be a sign of high blood pressure or pre-eclampsia (toxemia), which affects one in five first pregnancies.

🐚 Abdominal pain could be another sign of pre-eclampsia or miscarriage.

If you need extra rest time, take it. You need to conserve your energy for the birth.

Planning Ahead

If you have chosen not to work right up to the baby's arrival, use your new free time to plan ahead. There are things you—and your partner—can do now to bond with your baby, even before he is born, as well as making sure that the birth itself has the best chance of happening the way you would like. Think about baby equipment and nursery decorations, and enjoy the earliest days of new parenthood.

Getting to Know Your Baby

If your pregnancy seems to be rushing ahead without you, make some special time to quietly get to know your body and your baby. It's a great way to start bonding.

From the first time your felt your baby move—at around 17 weeks—you will have had an urge to keep touching your tummy. There's a biological reason for this: it's your instinctive need to bond with your unborn child. The great news is that, just as much as you love touching him, he loves feeling you do so. He's quickly getting to recognize your hand, as well as your partner's—and to respond to you. Some babies love being touched so much that they stick out their feet and hands to be rubbed.

From around 20 weeks the movements will become well-defined kicks, and when you sit in the bath, you can clearly see your baby move. Try pressing gently on the spot where you have just felt a kick and see if your baby responds with another one. And as your baby gets bigger, and you learn to identify different parts of his body (ask your midwife to show you if you're uncertain about what is what), try giving your baby a little massage by stroking the area covering his head, back, or bottom.

RELAX!

✿ Everyone keeps telling you to calm down—and there's a good scientific reason why you should do so. Research shows that when a pregnant mother is tense, her baby's heart rate increases and his movement patterns change. Other studies have shown that if you're overanxious, there's a greater likelihood of your baby being smaller than average and prone to hyperactivity. If you can make time to wind down and relax, you will be helping your baby's development—and, with luck, you will also produce a calmer child. What better excuse do you need for taking it easy?

Meditation is often said to be more energizing and beneficial than taking a short nap.

YOUR BABY LOVES

🐦 **SUGAR AND SPICE** He's already getting a taste for your favorite foods from the amniotic fluid. Spices like chili, garlic, and curry give the fluid a stronger flavor, and once he's born he will recognize your favorite foods in your breast milk, preferring the flavors he enjoyed in the womb. Babies have an inbuilt sweet tooth, and if you've been indulging your own sweet tooth, he will sip the sweetened amniotic fluid faster. Watch out—it could be a sign of things to come!

🐦 **EXERCISE** A good reason for keeping fit in pregnancy is that the feel-good hormones (endorphins) which give you a buzz do the same for your baby as they're passed to him across the placenta. He also gets a kick from your body moving around, which rocks him gently in the amniotic fluid.

🐦 **MUSIC** Mozart and Bach are thought to be particularly soothing: stretch your headphones across your bump and lull the baby to sleep.

...sic you enjoy will make your baby happy, too—introduce him to ...ur favorite tunes.

THINK POSITIVELY

🐦 If you feel anxious about the future, try to use positive visualization to turn your thoughts around and help you feel closer to your baby. For example, if you are overwhelmed by thoughts of the birth, sit comfortably, with your eyes closed, and imagine yourself holding your baby—and the lovely feelings you will have when this happens.

Your baby may have been able to hear your voice from as early as 12 weeks. Transmitted through your body, it's the easiest sound for him to detect, and talking soothingly or even repeating nursery rhymes to your bump may bring about another responsive kick (hopefully one of appreciation). You may feel a bit silly practicing baby talk so soon, but research shows that, even in the womb, a baby's heart rate slows down and he feels more rested when he hears you speak.

Babies are also fond of music with strong, regular beats, so play him your favorite song every day. Research shows that he'll recognize it after he's born, and may even be calmed by it—a useful tool if you want a quick soother.

Preparing for Birth

Ultimately, you may have little control over how long you will be in labor, and how smoothly it will go for you and your baby. However, there are steps you can take in late pregnancy to prepare yourself, and help the process—and if things still don't go quite as perfectly as you would have liked, you can at least reassure yourself that they could have been a whole lot worse if you hadn't acted so positively.

Getting ready

Your pregnancy may be the first time in your life you are introduced to herbal teas, massage, and relaxation. The following are all worth considering:

Feeling anxious about the birth is normal. Talk over any fears with your partner or your midwife.

PRIME YOUR BODY

The following exercises will help prepare your body for childbirth:

🦢 Squatting practice will help if you want to squat in labor. Squat down, keeping your back lengthened. If you can, keep your heels on the floor and balance your weight evenly between the balls of your feet and the heels, not letting your feet roll inward or outward. Always get up slowly, holding on to a chair or table, or you may feel dizzy.

🦢 Pelvic exercises will help you get comfortable in labor. Try the "lazy dog," kneeling on all fours, with a cushion under your knees if necessary. Move your pelvis from side to side like a lazy dog wagging a very heavy tail. Look round at each hip as you bring it forwards, and keep your back horizontal, not curved or caving.

Raspberry leaf tea is the classic recommendation for childbirth preparation. It strengthens and tones the uterus, making it more flexible for labor. But only drink it (up to three times a day) in the last trimester of pregnancy, as it has been known to overstimulate the uterus.

Massage can prepare the perineum (the area linking your private parts), making the area more supple for labor. Use wheatgerm or almond oil daily after a warm bath, in the last eight weeks of pregnancy.

Relaxation, practiced regularly, will prepare you for a more relaxed labor. Lie on your back on the floor, and, starting with your pelvis, take one body part at a time, tense it pressing into the floor, and then relax it. When your whole body is relaxed, your mind should slow down, too.

Aromatherapy oils such as mandarin and orange blossom are calming at this point in your pregnancy; and the homeopathic remedy Caulophyllum (blue cohosh) can be taken from 37 weeks to strengthen contractions and soften the cervix for an easier delivery.

Of course, many women go through pregnancy without doing any of these things—and they still have easy labors and healthy babies. Just do what feels right for you.

ARE YOU READY?

Fewer than ten percent of babies are premature, which means labor begins before Week 37, and, as most of these babies are born to women already thought to be at high risk, you will probably be prepared for this eventuality. But even if you are sailing through a perfectly normal and healthy pregnancy, with no risk factors, there's a very small chance your baby could arrive early—and the following symptoms must be taken seriously:

- Menstrual-like cramps.
- Lower back pain.
- Achiness in the pelvic floor, thighs, or groin.
- A change in your vaginal discharge (especially if it's watery or bloody).
- Broken waters—a trickle or rush of fluid from your vagina.

You may make friends for life at your childbirth classes, and your baby's new friends could be lying right by you!

CHILDBIRTH CLASSES

Be sure to choose a class that suits you. The main methods are:

- Bradley—which focuses on exercises to prepare your muscles for birth and your breasts for feeding. It places strong emphasis on the role of the partner in the childbirth experience, and on natural childbirth, encouraging women to avoid medical intervention unless absolutely necessary.
- Lamaze—uses relaxation and breathing techniques to fight pain, combined with an element of conditioning so that you respond to contractions in a way that will help rather than hinder your labor.

Writing a Birth Plan

A birth plan may seem like an excellent idea—you can spend time thinking about who you want with you at the birth, where you want to be (at home or in hospital), what you want to be doing (lying, bathing, or moving around), whether you want music in the background, or aromatherapy oils in the air—and, in case you don't feel strong enough to assert yourself in labor, you will have it all written down in black and white, so that your midwife and birthing partner can carry out your wishes.

However, as many women discover, having a birth plan that, in the end, does not go according to plan can cause huge disappointment. So probably the best advice anyone can give you is, "Be flexible!" Yes, you hope for a natural delivery with no pain relief; yes, you would like to be at home, with the midwife you have come to know throughout your pregnancy—but, ideally, yes, you will also be able to

accept that your midwife is caught up in her own crisis, a sudden problem means you're safer in hospital, and you're not as stoic as you thought when it comes to going without pain relief.

Your plan

When making a birth plan, think about the following:

🐾 Who would you like to be with you for the birth?

🐾 Do you want your partner to stay with you in the eve of a Cesarean or forceps delivery?

🐾 Do you want to bring in any special equipment such a beanbag or birthing chair?

🐾 Can you choose the way your baby's heart is monitored during labor?

🐾 Do you want to be treated by women only?

🐾 If yours is a teaching hospital, will you mind if medica students are present?

🐾 Do you want the freedom to move around in labor?

🐾 Is there a special position you'd like to use for delivery?

🐾 Do you plan to manage without pain relief?

🐾 Do you want to use aromatherapy oils?

🐾 Do you want music in the background?

🐾 Do you want a birthing pool?

🐾 Are you planning to use any alternative therapies for labor?

🐾 Do you want your baby cleaned before he's handed to you?

🐾 Are there any special religious customs you want to be observed?

Set aside time to plan ahead for the birth—and make sure you thi carefully about your wish list.

HAVING YOUR BABY AT HOME?

PROS

ℰ❧ You can do things your own way.

ℰ❧ You can be with your family.

ℰ❧ Your partner can participate fully.

ℰ❧ You're more relaxed and the baby will be less traumatized.

CONS

ℰ❧ It's not always suitable—for example, if you develop high blood pressure, it is likely to mean a hospital birth after all.

ℰ❧ Late transfer to hospital may become necessary if your labor needs help.

ℰ❧ If you do have to be transferred to hospital, it could be traumatic.

My Birth Plan

Use this page to write your own plans for delivery

....

....

....

....

....

....

....

....

....

....

....

....

....

....

....

....

Things to Look Into

When you're planning ahead, it's useful to set aside a list of important contacts for the birth and beyond. Think about the following issues involved in the various birth options.

Hospital birth

If you're planning a hospital birth, and are happy to go with the flow—accepting the doctor's or midwife's advice on the day—then all you may need to do now is draw up a final list of questions (to raise at an prenatal appointment) about the hospital staff (e.g. How many nurses are there on the unit? What hours do they work? What happens if a shift finishes while you're still in labor? What is the hospital's current policy on pain relief?). If you have not already been given the opportunity to do so, ask if you can have a tour of the maternity unit. It's helpful to know where you will be giving birth and where you will be before and afterward.

Home birth

If you're planning a home birth there's much more to arrange and some research to do, too. Where will you give birth? Will you be able to reach the bathroom easily? Is the room big enough for your attendees? If you are hoping to get to know your midwife in advance, this is an issue to rai at your prenatal clinic. You may find that your pregnancy i considered too high risk for a home birth. If this happens to you, you can ask your doctor or midwife to explain in writing why they feel this to be the case.

Water birth

Many women having their babies at home like the idea of doing so in a birthing pool, which has the advantage of being relaxing as well as helping to reduce pain and the risk of tearing. Do your research to find ou where you can hire or buy a birthing pool, and which type of pool is best suited to yo and your home. Important issues are the size of the pool and the ease of connectio to your hot water system. Many hospitals also offer birthing pools, but if you are afraid that it will not be available when yo want it (because it's in use by someone els or being cleaned), bringing in your own po

Giving birth at home can be comforting for som but it requires a lot of preparation in advance.

PLANNING FOR EXTRA HELP

In many cultures it's usual for new moms to dedicate the first few weeks of their new baby's life to bonding. They are expected to do no more than cuddle up with their child while other family members rally around, feeding and looking after them. To make this a more practical reality for you, look into the option of engaging paid help:

❧ A doula is an experienced woman whose job is to "mother the mother"—enabling you to make the most of your early days as a new mom. She can attend the birth (alongside a midwife or doctor) and offer emotional and practical postpartum support, working hours to suit your family and enabling you to have a rest period of up to 40 days.

❧ A night nurse who specializes in postpartum care can give a new mom a chance to get a good night's sleep. Typically she would be hired to help in the first four to eight weeks with night feeds (if the baby's using a bottle) and can help you and your baby settle into a routine at home. Talk to your doctor or hospital, or contact a home healthcare agency in your area.

❧ If you can afford it, get a part-time housekeeper to do cleaning chores, food preparation, and shopping.

Getting extra help during the first few weeks after delivery gives you time to devote yourself to your baby.

may be an option (check first). If a water birth is a high priority for you, be sure to make your midwife is aware of this during your prenatal clinic sessions.

Birthing centers

These are small maternity units, staffed and run by midwives, and they offer a comfortable, low-tech environment where your delivery will be treated as a normal process rather than a medical procedure. You're more likely to receive one-to-one treatment in a birthing center than in a hospital, and you will also have access to a range of facilities that may not be available in hospital, such as birthing pools, soft mats, flexible furniture—and, most important, a friendly and unhurried midwife!

Buying for Baby

Whether you choose to buy your equipment in advance of the birth, or wait until afterward, the same time-consuming research will be needed—so give yourself a good head start.

Transporting your baby

🐦 A car seat is your first priority, as you'll need it from day one.

🐦 Don't compromise by buying used items. Most damage isn't visible to the naked eye.

🐦 Remember that more expensive doesn't necessarily mean safer.

🐦 Have the seat professionally fitted. As many as 80 percent of child car seats are unsafe due to incorrect fitting by parents.

🐦 Check how long the seat will last your baby—first seats go from birth to 28-40 lb/13-18 kg.

🐦 Some seats let your baby lie flat.

🐦 Look into ease of cleaning.

🐦 A lightweight stroller may be a better option than a travel system with components that you will use for only the first three months. Choose one that's suitable from birth, comfortable for a newborn, and easy to fold and carry. As long as it's good quality, it should last a good two years.

🐦 A sling is useful and a cheaper option for young babies—if you plan to use one a lot, be prepared to pay extra for features that will give more support for your back, and more padding for your baby.

Sleep options

🐦 A moses basket is cute and comfortable for your new baby, but remember it will be used for only about two months—so it isn't worth paying too much.

🐦 A crib is an essential that will last for years, especially if you choose one that can be turned into a bed. Most

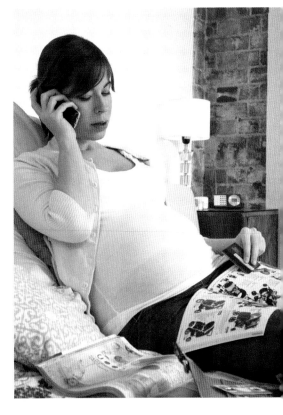

Catalogs are a great way to do your research, as well as saving you from trekking around the shops.

important is the mattress—growing spines need the best support available, so make this a priority in your budget. Don't buy a used mattress, as old mattresses can harbor harmful bacteria.

Monitoring your baby

🐦 Baby monitors vary a great deal in price. Make sure the one you choose suits your lifestyle. It needs a wide enough range for you to hear your baby wherever you are your home. Other features—such as a video screen, or talk back and music options—are luxuries.

Baby hygiene

✷ Diapers are a big outlay. In five months you will ʋe spent as much on disposable diapers as you would an initial reusable diaper supply. Look into other, less ensive options.

✷ A baby bath is useful and inexpensive, but not an sential item of equipment.

✷ A changing unit (also known as a changing table or tion) enables you to organize all your baby's changing aphernalia in one place, and is a good option if you have ck problems and would find it difficult to change your oy on the floor. However, it is a big, bulky, often expensive ce of furniture that takes up considerable space.

✷ A changing bag is not essential—you can use a carrier g and a towel if you need to—but, if you do buy one, nember you will be using it for at least two years, so look a design you won't tire of, and make sure it can be used e-handed if you're opening it while holding your baby in other arm.

A baby bath is an inexpensive piece of equipment that enables you to wash your infant safely at a practical height.

Basic equipment can be just as good as luxurious brands if you shop carefully.

MAKING ENDS MEET

✷ Prioritize buying the baby car seat, crib, and stroller or carriage.

✷ Put money aside from early in your pregnancy—a few dollars a week will soon add up.

✷ Have a baby shower—it can be a serious money saver, and you can draw up a list, like a wedding gift list, of the things you want or need for your baby.

✷ Don't always buy new—although some things like car seats and mattresses should be purchased new, most other items can be found in good condition used.

✷ Borrow some things from friends—they will have homes to go back to when you've finished with them.

Decorating a Nursery

You don't have to spend a fortune to create a lovely room for your baby—but you do have to make sure it is cozy, welcoming, practical, and safe. It must also be safe for you to prepare. Remember that many old paints contain lead, which is highly toxic—so stripping old paint (especially if it dates back to the 1970s) is a job you must hand over to someone else. Modern paint is lead-free, but you can also choose low-odor paint (which won't leave lingering fumes for your baby), and eco-paints made from organic materials which are also less harmful to the environment.

PINK OR BLUE?

❧ There's a biological reason why girls prefer pink and boys prefer blue—it's down to our hunter-gatherer days when women were the prime gatherers and needed an inbuilt radar for ripe, red fruits. That won't be an issue for your baby, but you may still be strongly tempted to decorate the room in cute baby blue or pink—which is great for their early years. But if you want a room that will grow with your child for a few more years before you have to start all over again, go for a neutral cream or pale green. A fancy wallpaper border can brighten up a plain-colored room, and is cheap and easy to change when you want a new look.

Don't feel pressured into preparing a nursery—especially if your baby will be sleeping in your room in the early weeks.

Keep it cozy

Make sure your baby's room is well heated and ventilated. Ideally it should be light and airy and very near your own room. Use a blackout lining in curtains or blinds to keep it cozy through shorter summer nights. A room thermometer is a good idea so you can check that the nursery remains a steady 68-72°F/20-22°C at night.

MAKE IT YOURSELF

If you enjoy crafts, your baby is the perfect excuse to get out your sewing kit.

➴ Make a double-thickness reversible fleece blanket. Start with lengths of fleece fabric in two contrasting colors—e.g. cream and pale blue or cream and pale pink. Have enough fabric to cut out a monogram from each piece, and still have enough left over to make a blanket that will fit your baby's crib. Cut soft-edged monograms, as fleece is not suitable for sharp corners. Cut the blanket pieces to size, and baste the monograms in place (color on cream and vice versa), then finish with a neat blanket stitch in cream-colored embroidery silk. Baste both pieces together approximately 1 inch/2.5 cm from the outside edges, then trim the cream layer about ½ inch/1.25 cm smaller than the blue. Fold the edge of the blue around the cream layer to form a mock binding, and finish it off with blanket stitch edging in cream embroidery silk.

....

➴ A laundry bag will be very useful. Make your own using pure cotton fabric that's easy to throw into the washing machine whenever necessary. Use enough fabric to make a large pillow case, and decorate it with appliqué flowers, numbers, or letters. Fold the raw edges of the opening over and stitch to make a drawstring top.

....

➴ Make your own mobile, cutting out shapes from craft foam, colored paper, or thin card. Hang these from an old wire coat hanger (you can reshape it first) using beading thread.

....

➴ Paint a large storage box to coordinate with the room, and decorate it with playful pictures to make a toybox.

BEST BUYS

➴ A dropside crib.
➴ Room thermometer.
➴ Comfy nursing or rocking chair for you.
➴ A chest of drawers.

➴ Washable flooring and nonslip rugs.
➴ A toybox.
➴ A good light with a dimmer switch for the night.
➴ A clothes rack or towel rack.

Baby Basics

Even newborn baby clothes now come in a range of sizes—shop carefully, bearing in mind your baby's estimated size (ask your midwife). If you're anticipating having a very small baby, you could end up rolling the sleeves of regular size garments right up to the shoulders. If your baby is likely to be big, consider that he may be bulging out of the same size suit after only a couple of wears. It's important not to put your baby in clothes that are too tight, as his bones will be soft and easily damaged if they're constricted.

Artificial materials, being non-porous, are great for top wear and sleeping bags, but wool and cotton mixtures provide more softness and warmth for onesies and stretch suits that will be next to your baby's skin.

Most babies are put into stretch suits day and night while they're tiny. If you prefer nighties (useful for speedy night-time diaper changes when you'll want to keep everything low-key so you can all get back to sleep quickly), go for a raglan style to allow for optimum freedom of movement and growth. Buttons and snaps are safer than ties, strings, and ribbons on onesies.

BASIC WARDROBE

ॐ Three or four onesies with an easy stretchy opening for the head, in cellular cotton or wool and cotton mix.

ॐ Three or four terry stretch suits for day and night wear.

ॐ Two or three matinée jackets or cardigans, with raglan sleeves.

ॐ Two sleeping bags suitable for wearing over a stretch suit at night (to stop him kicking off blankets and getting cold).

ॐ Four to six portable crib sized flannelette sheets (or crib size if you are not going to use a moses basket or portable crib).

ॐ Two or three cellular blankets.

ॐ Bibs for wiping dribbles and vomit.

ॐ Diapers.

ॐ A hat (cotton or fleece, according to the season/temperature).

Shopping for baby clothes and other essentials is a fun way to bond with a pregnant friend.

Keeping baby clean

any experts recommend that you use no chemicals at
 on a newborn baby, so look for natural products that
 ll be gentle on the baby's skin. Calendula products are
 rticularly good for a baby's skin (find them in health food
 ores). You will also need:

- Two or three soft hooded towels.
- A soft flannel.
- One or two soft toweling changing mats.

BABY'S HOSPITAL BAG

ITEM	YES
Onesies	
Stretch suits	
Hat	
Oversuit or cardigan for traveling home in	
A packet of first-size diapers	
Bibs	

Baby Buys

Use this space to keep a check of the baby basics you've stocked up on

Gifts

Item
....

From .... Thank you card sent ....

Item
....

From .... Thank you card sent ....

Item
....

From .... Thank you card sent ....

Item
....

From .... Thank you card sent ....

Item
....

From .... Thank you card sent ....

Item
....

From .... Thank you card sent ....

Item
....

From .... Thank you card sent ....

Item
....

From .... Thank you card sent ....

Item
....

From .... Thank you card sent ....

Item
....

From .... Thank you card sent ....

Loaned Items

Item
....

From   Thank you card sent

Item
....

From   Thank you card sent

Item
....

From   Thank you card sent

Item
....

From   Thank you card sent

Item
....

From   Thank you card sent

Item
....

From   Thank you card sent

Item
....

From   Thank you card sent

Item
....

From   Thank you card sent

Item
....

From   Thank you card sent

What's in a Name?

Your choice of baby name is one of the most important decisions you will make–after all, you (and he or she) will be stuck with it for a very long time! If you'd rather not have a child with a name that causes a stampede when you call it in the playground (as you will one day!), here are some tips to get your ideas flowing.

Sound it out

Practice saying baby names out loud, attached to your surname. Are they cumbersome and awkward, harsh, or melodious? Do they sound dignified or childish? Your child will be stuck with this name for life–or at least, you hope he won't want to change it as soon as he's old enough.

When you're thinking about the sound of a name, it's worth remembering that longer first names often work best with shorter surnames and vice versa. A first name that ends in a vowel–Bruno, Milo, Amelia, or Jessica, for example–doesn't go so well with a surname that also starts with a vowel; it's also a bad idea to have your child's first and surnames rhyming–e.g. Mike Pyke or Jane Payne. Think about how the name will sound on your child in adulthood, too, and avoid puns like Teresa Green, Holly Wood, and Wendy House.

Make it special

Is it unique? An unusual name will make your child more memorable than a common one–do you want him always to be known as Charlie A or Charlie B? However, if it's so unusual that people have never heard of the name before, or can't pronounce it, your child could be in for years of embarrassment every time he has to give his name and then repeat it and spell it out.

What are your relatives called? Explore old family names to see if there's one you'd like to resurrect. Names from our grandparents' or great-grandparents' generations have become popular for our own babies–think of Jack and Jacob, Amy and Lucy. Nancy and Edith are gaining popularity for girls, too.

Do you want a name with religious or historical significance? In France it's common to give a child the name of the saint associated with the day of his birth. Some families have a custom of passing on the same name to all firstborn sons. Or you may have some other special reason based on your own life to call your child a certain name–a hobby may inspire you, for example.

Do you want to give your child an alternative name? Sometimes it's best to keep the wackier names you come up with as middle names–your child still has the option of using that name in later life if it suits his character better than his first name. Likewise, if you choose to call your baby by a very outlandish name, why not give him something more traditional as a second name to fall back on?

A lot to live up to?

If you think your baby's name could affect his personality, check out the multitude of books that offer the meanings of names. For example, did you know that Amelia means "hardworking," while Antonia is "priceless," Winston is "joy," and Ziggy means "to get rid of anger"?

Take a minute to check that you're not calling your child anything that could be embarrassing when their initials are marked on their sports bag. Jane Olivia Young is lovely, but Freya Amanda Thomas is not!

Think about nicknames. Could your child's name be shortened to anything potentially embarrassing to your child? And, if you are giving your child a name such as Sir, Junior, or Hero, think hard about how they will cope with living with it.

Top 10 names

Boys	Girls
Jacob	Emily
Michael	Emma
Joshua	Madison
Ethan	Isabella
Matthew	Ava
Daniel	Abigail
Christopher	Olivia
Andrew	Hannah
Anthony	Sophia
William	Samantha

My favorite names

Baby Planner

Things I need to buy

....

....

....

....

....

....

....

....

....

....

....

Questions for my doctor

....

....

....

....

....

....

....

Baby Planner

Pre-baby arrangements

Special Information & Arrangement

For me

For baby

For partner

Special Information & Arrangements

For pets

For relatives

Meals for the freezer

Giving Birth

The birth itself is a voyage into the unknown. You can ask a hundred different women how it was for them—and you will get a hundred different stories. For some it is easy and quick; for others it is long and arduous. You can only wait and see how your delivery will be. The tips in the last chapter have helped you prepare for the birth; now find out what you can expect on your own big day.

Going into Labor

You may have mixed feelings about labor. It's the time your baby's arrival is finally imminent but none of us can foresee how quick and easy, or long and complicated, the process will be.

Throughout your pregnancy you will have had occasional practice contractions, known as Braxton Hicks contractions. As your due day approaches, these become stronger and more frequent. Pre-labor symptoms, which can start a full month before the real thing—or sometimes only an hour before—include:

🐦 Crampiness in the pelvis and rectum.

🐦 Persistent low backache.

🐦 A change in energy levels—for better or worse.

EARLY LABOR

Whether you're at home or in hospital for the earliest stage of your labor, try to stay relaxed—it will help with the delivery. This is a good time to use the relaxation exercises you learned in the last chapter.

🐦 It's a good idea to eat high-energy foods such as pasta, bananas, or toast and honey, but check with your midwife or doctor as labor progresses that she's happy for you to continue eating and drinking.

🐦 A warm bath can be comforting in early labor. Add essential oils of clary sage and frankincense to the water, mixed into an unscented bubble bath base. Clary sage will tone your uterus and strengthen contractions. Frankincense is good for deepening your breathing, which will help you relax.

🐦 Walking around can help with the pain of contractions, and squatting on a small stool between them will help open the pelvis.

IT'S LIKELY TO BE THE REAL THING IF:

🐦 Your contractions are intensifying and changing position doesn't help.

🐦 Your contractions become more frequent and painful.

🐦 You've had a bloody show—a pink or bloody discharge as the cervix effaces and dilates, rupturing capillaries.

🐦 Your waters have broken.

If you think you could be in labor, call your doctor or midwife straightaway. They'll tell you what to do next. Don't be put off by fear of embarrassment in case it's not labor after all—and don't delay too long unless you've planned a home birth! Even though the start of labor may herald a long wait, it's an unpredictable process and you must be prepared for a short labor, too.

Your partner's support through labor will be a comfort, and helps both parents to feel involved in the birth process.

member the calming yoga or breathing exercises you have been
ght. They can become invaluable during labor.

DO TRY THIS AT HOME

**Here's a simple breathing exercise that will help you
to relax:**

🐋 Inhale slowly through one nostril, closing the
other by pressing a finger against it. As you breathe
in, feel your diaphragm gently rise to your chest.
Breathe out, very slowly, through the opposite
nostril while keeping the first one closed. As you
exhale, imagine you're sending your breath through
every part of the body. Continue until you feel
calmer and more relaxed.

GETTING THINGS MOVING

If labor is slow to start, try the following:

🐋 **EAT CURRY** Spicy foods are great if your
baby's overdue as they have a similar (though
not so fierce) effect to old-fashioned castor oil,
stimulating the bowels, which in turn will help
trigger the start of labor (though nobody knows
exactly why).

🐋 **MAKE LOVE**—semen contains natural
prostaglandin. In hospital you'd probably be
given synthetic prostaglandin to induce labor.

🐋 **USE GRAVITY** In early labor, being upright
and moving around as much as possible will help
things along by encouraging the baby's head
down, and exerting more pressure on the cervix.
Go for a walk, or even dance around the house
a little. Being upright encourages a good flow of
blood and oxygen to the baby, enabling her to stay
in good condition through the labor.

🐋 **DIM THE LIGHTS** Your body needs to
feel safe, secure, and relaxed before the birth
hormones can really start working and labor can
proceed unhindered.

🐋 **HAVE YOUR NIPPLES STIMULATED** Here's
something for your partner to do. Stroking or
massaging the nipples helps trigger the release
of the hormone oxytocin, which helps move
labor along. In trials, nipple stimulation has
been proved more effective than pitocin, the
synthetic hormone administered by injection
to induce contractions.

How Long Will It Last?

How long will your labor last? The tempting answer to that is the age-old question: "How long is a piece of string?" It can be amazingly quick—some women do not even register that they're in labor until they are ready to deliver. On the other hand, as friends will tell you, it can also be laboriously slow. But you can be in labor for more than 20 hours as a first-time mom before it officially counts as a "long labor," or more than 14 hours if you have had a baby before.

Labor is divided into three stages, and, just to confuse you more, the first of these stages is divided into two subsections: early labor (when you're up to 4 cm dilated—see pages 70-71), and active labor (when you're 4-10 cm dilated). Your cervix must be 10 cm dilated before you are ready to deliver your baby, and this is what your midwife or doctor will be closely monitoring. Even if you have an urge to push, she will ask you to resist until you really are ready.

It's important to feel you can trust the midwife or doctor who is looking after you during all the stages of labor.

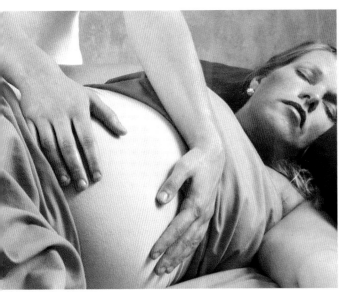

Active labor (part of stage 1)

During active labor, your uterus contracts to pull the cervix over the baby's head; it also moves forward to push your baby down hard on the cervix, where the pressure of her head helps it to open. The more relaxed you are, the better your uterus will work. Active labor lasts, on average, between five and seven hours—but there are many variations. For instance, the uterus can achieve more in less time if contractions become stronger, longer, and more frequent (three to four minutes apart and lasting for 40-60 seconds). Each contraction should have a distinct peak, but they may not be as regular as you'd expected.

Stay as upright as you can and lean forward, never backward. Kneeling over a beanbag or pile of pillows can be comfortable, or try leaning into your partner's arms. Going on all fours is very popular and allows you to rock from side to side during a contraction. Your partner can also reach your back easily if you want it stroked or massaged.

Relaxing in your partner's arms is a lovely way to go through labor—and a more likely eventuality if you are giving birth at home, or in a birthing center.

This is the time to focus on your breathing to stop yourself tensing against the pain. Breathe out through your mouth—sighing or groaning deeply helps a lot.

Transition

At the end of active labor, you will feel an irresistible urge to push down. This is when your doctor or midwife will give you a vaginal examination to check that you're almost 10 cm dilated. As soon as you are, you will be allowed to start pushing.

Birth (stage 2)

Many women get a helpful second wind that eases them through the pushing phase of labor. Choose your pushing position and get comfortable—semi-sitting, squatting, or kneeling on all fours puts gravity on your side to help things along. Listen carefully to your body and, when you feel like pushing, give it your all. Your baby's head will stretch the skin of your perineum and emerge, followed by the shoulders and the rest of the body. This may take several contractions, but the doctor or midwife's hands will be close to make sure she comes out safely. Another advantage to being on all fours is that you're less likely to tear.

If you are pushing for longer than two hours, or three hours with an epidural, your doctor may want to use forceps or perform a Cesarean section to get the baby out—but if steady, though slow, progress is being made, and both you and the baby are doing well, then a natural vaginal delivery should still be able to go ahead.

Delivering the placenta (stage 3)

After the birth of your baby, your uterus continues to contract strongly to expel the placenta. You may be asked to push against the doctor or midwife's hand, placed on your lower abdomen, while she gently pulls on the umbilical cord with her other hand.

Pain Relief

Reading a raw account of the stages of labor, it is hard to imagine how you and your body will actually cope with the real event—and pain relief is a burning issue for most moms-to-be. A number of factors influence the pain level of labor, including the size and position of the baby, the strength of uterine contractions, and your own pain tolerance. No woman can predict what sort of pain she'll have during labor or how she'll cope with it. Try to keep an open mind about what your needs might be.

Do ask your prenatal clinic about the pain relief available in your area—it is possible to get to hospital assuming that you will be offered certain drugs, only to find that the latest policy discourages their use. Which method you decide to use (if any at all) depends on your preference, your health care provider's recommendations, and the availablity at your birthing facility. The options you may be offered include narcotics, epidural anesthesia, and spinal block.

Things to consider before choosing

- What's involved in the method?
- How will it affect me?
- How will it affect my baby?
- How quickly will it work?
- How long will the pain relief last and can I combine it with other methods of pain relief?
- At what stage during labor is the method available?

Narcotics

These are considered to be the next step up from the natural methods of pain relief such as relaxation exercises deep breathing, massage, and laboring in water. Narcotics are morphine-like drugs that are administered in small doses in early labor, before you start pushing. Narcotics ar

Knowing what kind of pain relief is available will make you feel more confident about the birth.

NATURE'S WAY

🐋 Water stimulates natural pain-relieving endorphins and supports your weight.

🐋 The breathing exercises taught in prenatal classes are one of the most basic, but most effective, ways of dealing with pain.

🐋 Hot and cold compresses can ease pain in your lower back.

have a combined spinal/epidural during childbirth, which offers the advantages of rapid pain relief of the spinal block along with the continuous pain relief of the epidural.

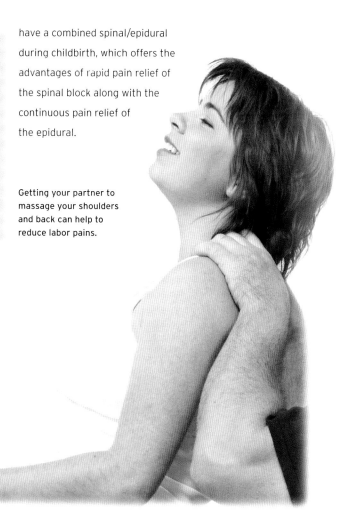

Getting your partner to massage your shoulders and back can help to reduce labor pains.

...t-acting and can take the edge off painful contractions, ...aking you feel relaxed and less aware of the pain. However ...ey can also make you feel sick and sleepy, and less aware ...the labor. A narcotic will also cross through the placenta ...your baby, who may (rarely) need an injection after birth ...reverse the effects of the drug.

Epidural

...is a procedure whereby medication is injected into your ...ver back, to numb the nerves carrying pain signals from ...ur womb to your brain, and deliver continuous pain relief. ...dication is generally a combination of local anesthetic ...d narcotic, administered via a tube that's threaded ...rough a hollow needle into your back. it takes about 20 ...nutes for the procedure to take effect. Although over ...percent of women get complete pain relief from the ...dural, and your mind remains clear throughout, you will ...ve to stay in bed, and it can be harder to push, making a ...ceps or ventouse delivery more likely. You may also need ...atheter as you won't necessarily feel the urge to urinate.

Spinal block

...is a one-off injection delivered directly into the spinal ...d, and is usually given if pain relief is required at a late ...ge of labor. Pain relief is rapid and complete but only ...ts a few hours. Nowadays it is becoming common to

ALTERNATIVE THERAPIES

🐋 Aromatherapy can make the birth easier and reduce pain: a bath or massage with a few drops of clary sage essential oil will help labor along.

🐋 Acupuncture will relax you and stimulate the release of natural endorphins, but will necessitate the presence of a trained acupuncturist.

🐋 Homeopathy can help with minor complications in labor. For unbearable pain during transition, take Chamomilla. Bryonia can help with pain made worse by any movement or touch.

Assisted Deliveries

Many women need medical help to deliver their baby safely. Methods employed include forceps, vacuum suction, and Cesarean section.

Cesarean section

A Cesarean section may be recommended early in your pregnancy because of some known complication, in which case you will be given a date and will know exactly when you are having your baby. An emergency Cesarean is carried out when a problem is identified during labor. Even if you've had a hitherto problem-free pregnancy, a Cesarean can become necessary—and many women wish they'd been better prepared, having not read up on the procedure because they'd assumed it wouldn't happen to them.

In fact, about one in three women arriving in hospital to have their first baby will undergo an emergency Cesarean

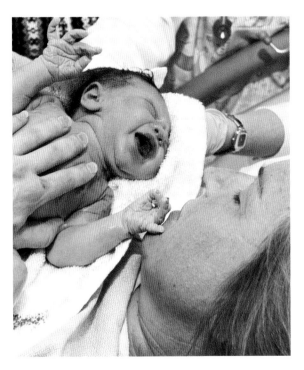

section. The word "emergency" can be alarming but most unplanned Caesareans are not carried out in life-threatening circumstances. In 40 percent of cases, the decision is taken because labor is progressing more slowly than expected, or because the baby is showing signs of distress.

Even though this is an operation, you still have choices available to you—and a Cesarean birth can still be a wonderful experience. If you have the operation carried out under epidural, you will be able to see your baby as soon as she is born, and this is very important for some women who feel they'd be missing out on the birth if they were unconscious. You can ask for the screen to be removed or lowered so you can watch the operation if you want to, and you can also ask for a member of staff or your partner to take photos or a video. These pictures will be precious to you if you have had a general anesthetic and feel you were rendered "absent" from your own delivery.

If your baby is well, and most are, she can be wrapped in a blanket and laid across your shoulder so you and your partner can enjoy her company for the first time while you are being sewn up. You can also, if you want, have skin-to-skin contact with your baby or breastfeed in the theater or recovery room.

Helping baby out

If it is discovered in labor that your baby is lying obliquely or transversally, the force of the contractions may push the presenting part—shoulder, arm, or leg—down into the birth canal and the umbilical cord may be the first thing to drop into the vagina once the waters have gone. This is a very dangerous situation and means the baby cannot be delivered vaginally, and you'll need a Cesarean section.

Having a Cesarean section doesn't have to mean missing out on the moment when your baby is born.

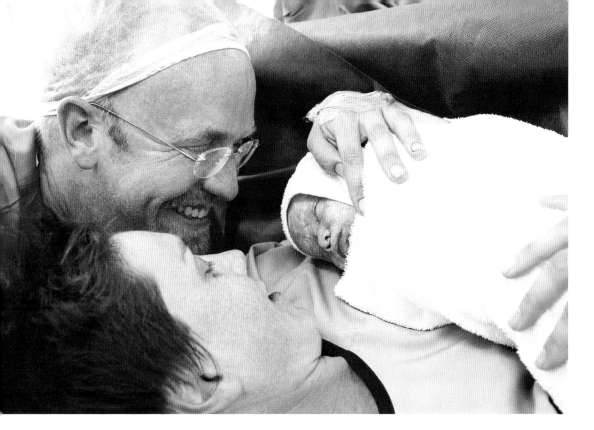

The first cuddle is another of those special moments that new parents will remember forever.

Forceps may be used to turn a baby's head if the presenting part is too wide to descend through the birth canal, or you're too tired to complete the delivery without help. You may also need forceps if the baby's distressed, or if there's a delay in the second stage of labor. When forceps are used, you'll be given a local anesthetic before the curved blunt blades are cradled one at a time around the baby's temples so she can be gently delivered.

Vacuum extraction is a popular alternative to forceps and involves suctioning the baby out of the birth canal with a cap which is applied to the head. It has the advantage that it can be used before the cervix is fully dilated, whereas forceps require full dilatation. Both vacuum and forceps can leave your baby's head looking swollen and bruised, but this quickly subsides and rarely causes long-term harm.

If you have concerns about the possible use of forceps or vacuum extraction, discuss them with your doctor or midwife before labor.

CRANIAL OSTEOPATHY

Cranial osteopathy is often recommended for babies following a ventouse or forceps-aided delivery because colic, excessive crying, and sticky eyes in newborns are all aggravated by compression of the cranial bones during birth. The technique was first described by William Sutherland in 1899, who felt that gentle manual compression and tapping of the skull could improve the circulation of cerebrospinal fluid. The bones making up the skull are still soft and separate in babies and young children, and disturbances in the flow of cerebrospinal fluid due to birth trauma may be eased by cranial osteopathy. Treatment mainly involves gentle touching or tapping rather than obvious manipulation of the skull bones.

Hello, Baby!

When your baby is delivered all you may want to do is coo over her—so ask the doctor or midwife if you can spend some time with her before she gets on with the essential work of checking your baby over.

The cord is usually clamped and cut as soon as your baby is born, but this can be delayed until after the placenta has been delivered, if you hold your baby by your thigh, level with the placenta, until the cord is cut. Cutting the cord is a simple procedure and your partner may like to do it—ask ahead of time if this is what you want. A mucus extractor (a plastic tube inserted into the nostrils to suck out secretions) is sometimes used to clear blocked airways, but usually the mucus will drain naturally.

Midwives often ask if you'd like to put the baby straight to your breast. Some are born ready to suck, but don't worry

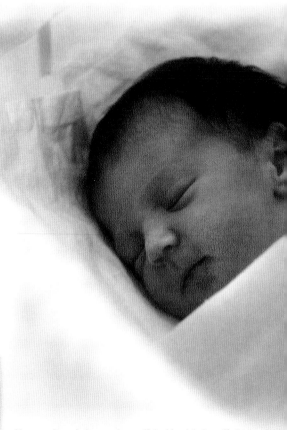

Your newborn baby may have slicked back hair as if she has just emerged from a swimming pool.

THE APGAR SCORE

Babies are checked and given a score (out of ten) for the following factors that make up the Apgar Score, named after the doctor who developed the assessment:

- Heart rate
- Breathing
- Skin color
- Muscle tone
- Reflex response

Each is given up to two points but a total of seven plus is considered fine when the baby is one minute old. At five minutes old, a baby should have a score of nine. Babies do not usually achieve a score of ten at one minute old, as it takes a few minutes to adjust to life outside the womb.

if yours isn't ready. Just let her lie close to your breast while she gets used to the idea. A baby's sucking can stimulate contractions to release the placenta—but don't try to force it if it doesn't feel right. Your nipples can be stimulated by hand, having the same effect on contractions.

Bonding

Some authorities say the best way to bond with your baby immediately after birth is to dim the lights and look into her eyes, observing the reaction you get. But this is not practical for all women—in an emergency situation for either the mother or child, for instance, the baby will be temporarily taken away. In any case, different women have different experiences of bonding. If you are at all worried that your feelings for your baby are not what you expected them to be, just talk to your midwife or doctor. Don't keep things to yourself, and never think of yourself as a failure.

Jaundice

Jaundice is very common in the first days of life, causing the baby to look slightly yellow. It's caused by a buildup of waste products in the baby's body while she's still unable to remove these properly. It's a waste product called bilirubin, from old red blood cells, that causes the yellow color. It's not usually serious, and frequent feeds will help flush the illness from the baby's system—however, if it takes a hold, the baby

In the early hours with your baby, sleep may be the last thing on your mind—but hospital staff may expect you to rest.

may need phototherapy, which involves her being placed naked under a special light that breaks down the bilirubin. Very high levels of bilirubin can damage the brain, so phototherapy treatment will always be started well before any dangerous level is reached. If your baby's jaundice hasn't cleared in two weeks, contact your doctor or midwife, who will arrange a blood test to find out why. Very rarely, baby jaundice is a sign of a liver problem.

Babies are born with a strong grasp reflex and can usually grip your finger tightly.

NEWBORN METABOLIC PANEL

❧ Around six days after birth your baby will have her first blood test—the Newborn Metabolic Panel. This tests primarily for two disorders: phenylketonuria (a metabolic disorder that can cause intellectual impairment if not controlled by a special diet) and thyroid deficiency (which can also lead to mental impairment but is treatable with thyroxine). This test may also be used to diagnose other disorders such as cystic fibrosis. If your baby was smaller than expected she may also be tested for hypoglycemia (low blood sugar level).

Why Weight Matters

One of the first things everyone will want to know about your baby is "How much did she weigh?". Our babies' weights at birth are etched in our memory forever—as if they were the first point of reference for their resumé. But does the size of your baby really matter?

Babies are considered normal and healthy if they weigh between 7 lb 8 oz (3.5 kg) and 9 lb 9 oz (4.5 kg). Where your

baby is on this scale (the average is now 7 lb 5 oz in the US depends on your own size and that of the baby's father—and if you are very small or very big your baby could be bigger or smaller than these parameters and still be perfectly normal and healthy for you and your family.

However, eight percent of babies weigh in at less than 5 lb 5 oz (2.5 kg), the official low birthweight figure, and their low weight can be a serious health issue. Neonatal deaths and stillbirths are more likely among tiny babies, and researchers have also found that children who are small at birth tend to perform less well at school. In later life these children are also more prone to heart disease, diabetes, and strokes.

Your baby's weight

If you are small and women in your family tend to have small babies, a below average weight baby may be normal for you. But low birthweight can be caused by poor nutrition in pregnancy—one reason why healthy eating is discussed at length in this book. Mothers of babies weighing less than 5 lb 8 oz (2.6 kg) have often lacked vital nutrients, including B vitamins, magnesium iron, zinc, and essential fatty acids. Smoking greatly increases the risk, and some studies have also linked caffeine with low birthweight babies. If you were below

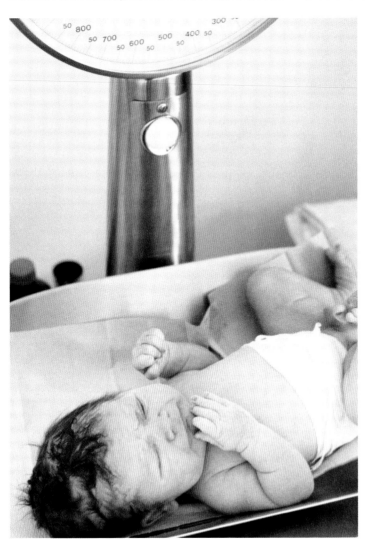

It's normal for babies to lose some of their newborn weight before they start gaining.

erage weight yourself when you became pregnant, this
uld also influence the weight of your baby when she is
orn—which is why your doctor will have weighed you at the
st prenatal appointment, and why underweight women
e generally encouraged to build themselves up before
tting pregnant.

At the other end of the scale, a baby who gains a
t of weight in the first week of life (when most babies
ruggle to put on weight as they're adjusting to their
w surroundings) is thought to be at greater risk of
esity in later life. Researchers found that for every
5 oz (100 g) gained, the risk of being overweight as
adult rose by 10 percent.

You're more likely to produce a big baby if you have
d gestational diabetes, which is caused by a failure in
sulin production to control the increase in blood sugar
vels that's triggered by hormonal changes. Gestational
abetes is a greater risk if you're overweight yourself.
aving a larger baby can cause problems with labor and
livery, and can increase your risk of needing a Cesarean
ction or forceps delivery.

Underweight babies are 50 percent more likely to
ffer from depression in later life, according to a study
Bristol University that charted the progress of 5,572
bies into adulthood, looking at mental development and
havioral problems.

Babies who were small at birth may need extra feedings to help
them put on weight in the first few weeks of life.

SMALL FOR DATES

ᘔᕼ Babies who appear not to be growing properly
in the womb may be suffering from intra-uterine
growth restriction—IUGR for short—which means
that the uterus is not adequately nurturing the baby.
Suspicions will have been raised early in the third
trimester and your pregnancy will have been closely
monitored until the birth.

"I WASN'T EXPECTING THAT!"

ᘔᕼ If you've had a late-pregnancy ultrasound scan, you
may have been reassured by being given your baby's
anticipated birth weight. It can be a shock, therefore, to
discover that your baby is much smaller than you were
led to believe—but in one study, ultrasound was found to
overestimate babies' weights by up to 1 lb (500 g) in
77 percent of the participants.

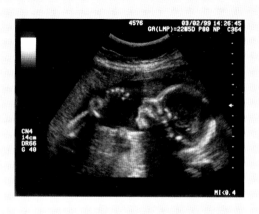

New Mom!

Congratulations—you're now a mom. The early hours and days will be a delight, but they can also be a complete shock to your system. For one thing, you have your own recovery to consider.

🌿 **CONTRACTIONS** Yes, you still have a few to come. These are known as afterpains, and are the result of the uterus returning to its normal size. They're common when the baby is feeding—the sucking stimulates them—and are normally stronger with second, third, or fourth babies than with your first.

TOP TIP: Herbal antispasmodic drops can help the process of getting your uterus back into shape and can relieve pain, too. They can be bought ready

made from herbal suppliers and you should take 10 to 20 drops in water just before breastfeeding. If you can't find ready made drops, try black cohosh or cramp bark, which are both available as tablets from health food stores.

Herbal remedies such as black cohosh (from Banberry the flower seen here) can act as pain relievers and help to get your uterus back into shape after labor.

🌿 **LOCHIA** is the name given to the vaginal bleeding you experience after childbirth. For the first 48 hours it's likely to be quite heavy—much heavier than any period you have experienced—and you will need to use large maternity pads. After the first two days the blood loss lessens, but altogether the lochia will continue for anything from two to six weeks after the birth.

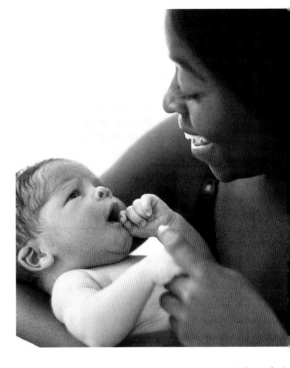

The joy of new motherhood usually eclipses any body discomforts you may be experiencing.

TOP TIP: You can control excessive lochia by applying pressure to a reflexology point just in front of the webbing between your big toe and the one next to it on the upper side of your right foot.

🌿 **BRUISING** is inevitable as your vagina has been stretched and the muscles worked hard during labor.

TOP TIP: Soak a sanitary pad in diluted tincture of calendula, which is very soothing. Freeze it, and wear it next to your skin until it thaws out.

🌿 **PAIN IN YOUR TAILBONE** (the coccyx) is also very likely, as it was pushed backward as the baby passed through the birth canal.

LIFE AFTER A CESAREAN

After a Cesarean, your body has to recover from two major traumas—childbirth and surgery. Be gentle on yourself. You need plenty of help—especially in the first week, when you shouldn't do any lifting or housework. Lift your baby with care. The homeopathic remedies arnica and calendula can speed up your recovery. If your Cesarean section was unplanned, take staphisagria. Acupuncture can also help to treat a Cesarean scar that is painful and slow to heal.

)P TIP: If it is very painful, take St John's Wort. Although is is best known as a natural antidepressant, herbalists so recommend it for chronic nerve pains and for trauma d injury involving nerve damage. If the problem lasts nger than a few days, an osteopath should be able to ieve it.

CONSTIPATION is likely in the first few days after ving birth, and is caused by heavy fluid loss, which normal (your body stored up a lot of excess fluid in egnancy and this is shed in the first few days after livery, in your urine, blood loss, and sweat). But it is st to try and avoid constipation if you can, as straining an already delicate and stretched area is extremely comfortable.

)P TIP: Drink plenty of water and make sure your diet rich in fiber—whole grains, fruit, and vegetables. Avoid xatives if you can, as they will be passed through your east milk to your baby.

Your partner's support is all the more important after a Cesarean section, when recovery can be slow.

IN STITCHES?

If you've had stitches for either a tear or an episiotomy, these can be quite uncomfortable for a few days. Soothing remedies such as arnica, or tincture of hypercal (put this on a sanitary pad) can help speed up healing and reduce soreness.

A healthy diet is a safe alternative to laxatives if you are constipated.

Baby's First Feeding

Whether you plan to feed your baby by breast or bottle is a very personal choice—and both have advantages. Either way, the first feeding is a lovely experience.

Breastfeeding

All through pregnancy your breasts have been preparing to feed your new baby—and most midwives and doctors will encourage you to breastfeed unless there is good reason not to (for example, if you have been very unwell and need to conserve energy for your own recovery). The first feeding can take place straight after birth—that's when babies' sucking reflexes are supposed to be at their strongest—and, when you see new moms do it on the TV, it looks like the simplest act on Earth.

Unfortunately it's not so straightforward for all of us. After all, both you and your baby are complete novices, so if it feels like the blind leading the blind, then it probably is—for now. The good news is that a midwife or hospital lactation specialist can help you both become accustomed to it. And even if you don't plan to breastfeed long term, you may be encouraged to at least try it for the first few days. This is when your breasts produce a special kind of pre-milk called colostrum, which is a transitional food, helping your baby move on from life in the womb to life in the big wide world. Colostrum provides a range of antibodies that will protect your baby from the diseases you've had and those that you have been immunized against. It is nutritionally so valuable that many people argue that all newborns should be given their mother's colostrum, even if mom intends to bottle feed afterward.

Trouble-shooting

The longer and more frequently your baby sucks, the sooner your milk will "come in"—until that time, colostrum supplies all the water and nourishment she needs. When your milk does come in (this can take a few days to happen), what may have developed into a happy and comfortable feeding pattern could suddenly become painful for you, and difficult for your baby if your breasts become swollen and hard—engorged. It shouldn't last too long, but, while it does, try to feed more often (for shorter periods) and don't be tempted to skip a feed because it hurts. Using a breast pump immediately prior to feeding may reduce the engorgement enough for your baby to get a better hold of the nipple so that the milk flow can start.

An old wives' tale, still frequently followed, suggests that putting bruised cabbage leaves on your engorged breasts has a natural anti-inflammatory effect. Taking echinacea tincture (15 drops in water) can prevent infection when you're engorged, and cold compresses and hot showers can both reduce the swelling.

Breastfeeding is a skill that you and your baby will have to learn together.

BREASTFEEDING BASICS

Make yourself comfy—a straight-backed chair with an armrest will help you get into the right position.

🐦 If your baby is swaddled, unwrap her so her arms are free to move around.

🐦 Hold her close, half-sitting her body toward yours, with her head in the crook of your arm.

🐦 Use your thumb and forefinger to pull your nipple erect.

🐦 Lean forward slightly, so that the nipple easily falls into her mouth.

🐦 Your baby gets the milk by taking your nipple deep into her mouth and pressing rhythmically on the milk sacs beneath the areola with her gums.

🐦 As she latches on, check that her jaws are well behind your nipple so she doesn't bite you (if she does, you'll be sore, and she's wrongly positioned to get her milk).

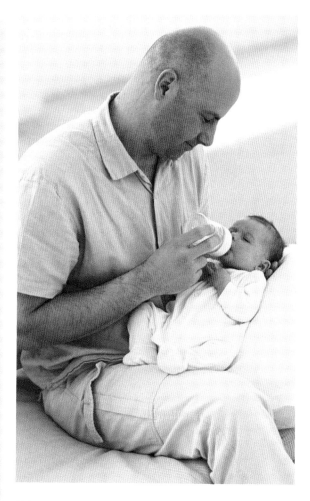

Giving a bottle can be a great way for fathers to bond with their babies, as well as giving the mother a break.

Use a breast pump to express breast milk—this can be frozen and reheated for the baby at a later date.

ml120• •4fl oz

90• •3

60• •2

30• •1

Bottle feeding

Babies find it easier to feed from a bottle—it takes less skill than breastfeeding, and, if your baby is offered a bottle early on, it may be difficult, though not impossible, to go back to breastfeeding. However, if you are not available for an early feed (for example, if you require some urgent postnatal medical treatment for a retained placenta or a hemorrhage—these things happen!), a bottle will be offered to your baby—and she will quickly acquire a taste for it. You can still get help with breastfeeding, or even mixing bottles and breast, if this is your choice.

Breast, Bottle, or Both?

There is probably nothing that divides mothers more than the issue of breast versus bottle feeding—and the arguments stretch way beyond the first year, too. Will breastfeeding make your baby a healthier child? Will bottle feeding help her into a good routine earlier on? If you choose to breastfeed, when should you stop? And if you do stop, should you ever switch to a bottle, or put your baby straight onto a sippy cup?

Ultimately, whether you choose to feed your baby with your own milk, formula, or a combination, is entirely your choice—but a lot of experts will urge you not to dismiss breastfeeding without at least giving it a try. Breastfeeding has great advantages for your baby (it provides everything she needs nutritionally) and for you (it is so convenient—assuming you're with your baby at the times she needs her feeds). The most difficult part of breastfeeding is usually the beginning, when you and your baby are learning how to do it. After that it gets easier and easier.

Although breastfeeding can be difficult to start with, most babies quickly become accustomed to it.

Breastfeeding

PROS

🐚 Your breasts have an amazing ability to manufacture according to season: in hot weather your milk will quench thirst without compromising on the food part of the feed.

🐚 Breast milk protects your baby from allergies, infections, and even obesity.

🐚 Your baby's diapers won't be as smelly as those of a formula-fed baby.

🐚 It's cheaper than feeding with a bottle.

🐚 It provides extra closeness, which adds to the bonding process between you and your baby.

CONS

🐚 Your breasts can leak and you can feel damp and smelly—even though your baby thinks you smell delicious!

🐚 You will need to express milk if you're away from your baby or back at work.

🐚 You may develop problems such as sore nipples, a blocked duct (causing a tender lump and feverishness), or mastitis (further inflammation).

DID YOU KNOW?

🐚 Breastfeeding enables you to eat more than you did pre-pregnancy—and still lose weight if you're active.

🐚 The hormone oxytocin, released during orgasm, is also released when you breastfeed, triggering a feeling of well-being.

🐚 Adults who were fed on breast milk as babies score higher in intelligence tests than those who were bottle fed.

Bottle feeding

PROS

- Someone else can help with feeds.
- You can be more independent.
- You take more control of the baby's routine.

CONS

- Babies are more likely to become overweight.
- There's an increased risk of gastroenteritis.
- Formula, although good for babies, does not offer all the added extras (immune protection, etc.) of breast milk.

MAKING UP BOTTLES

- Wash your hands before you start.
- Sterilize the bottles and use sterile plastic tongs to handle the teats to avoid bacterial infection.
- Boil fresh water for the bottle—don't reboil water left in the kettle. Leave it to cool for at least ten minutes, then pour it into the bottles.

many moms, the bottle is a more convenient option—and enables you to see exactly how much your baby is taking.

BOTH

PROS

You get the best of both worlds—the closeness of feeding your baby yourself, and the independence that comes with letting someone else give her a bottle to feed from.

CONS

Both baby and breasts will become confused and your breast milk supplies will dwindle. If you're planning to mix bottle and breast, it is best to do it when you're already trying to wind down breastfeeding in order to minimize the problems.

Mix up the bottle by adding the powdered formula to the water, not the other way round, and using a ratio of one level scoop (provided with the mix) to 2 tablespoons of boiled water.

Allow the formula to cool completely, then store in the fridge for up to 24 hours.

Warm the milk for feeding your baby by standing the bottle in a bowl of freshly boiled water for a few minutes.

Test the temperature on your wrist before offering it to your baby.

A bottle that hasn't been finished can be offered again within half an hour of first starting it. After that, throw it away and offer a fresh one.

This is what I did

....

....

....

Feeling Good

Becoming a mom is something you've been looking forward to for months, right? And your baby is the most beautiful sight in the world—even if she does have a funny shaped head, puffy eyes, and blotches. On paper you should be overjoyed, but a few days after birth it can suddenly seem that everything is wrong, even though nothing actually is. What you are experiencing is the "baby blues." It is more than an emotional reaction to the birth—it has a physical trigger, the change in hormone levels after delivery.

Throughout pregnancy, hormone levels rise to accommodate the baby and, by the time labor begins, levels of progesterone and estrogen are 50 times higher than they were before the pregnancy. After the birth, these levels fall suddenly and dramatically so that within hours they are below the levels they were at before the pregnancy began. The good news is that this feeling should pass within a few hours or, at the most, a few days.

In the meantime, you need to be given the freedom to cry and express your fluctuating emotions. If you feel miserable, you should not be told to pull yourself together, but instead listened to and reassured that the misery will soon pass. A mom with the blues is very sensitive to anything medical staff and friends and relatives may say—s tact and empathy are key words for carers at this time.

The baby blues or PPD

If your blues seem to be dragging on, get some profession. help. Midwives, doctors, and nurses know the symptoms of postpartum depression (PPD), which affects about one in ten new moms. They can help you get the support you need to pull through, but you will have to alert them to your feelings in the first place. Although some women will actually need psychiatric help and drugs for their depression, it's important to note that all cases of PPD do eventually pass—and you need not be separated from your baby during your illness and recovery.

Don't stress about keeping on top of the housework—just now, baby comes first.

DOING JUST GREAT

🐦 Don't try to do too much—make your baby your priority, and delegate household chores to someone else.

🐦 Let yourself be pampered. You need time to ease into your new role as mom. Look into hiring the help of a doula if you can afford it.

🐦 Get all the rest you can—you have big demands on your body if you are feeding a baby and getting up at night.

🐦 Eat well—make sure you get plenty of oily fish ("brain food") and sustaining whole foods (beans and whole grains) to supply essential B vitamins, which help keep your mood up.

🐦 Avoid "sugary" high glycemic index foods (including chips and white bread) and junk food, which will exacerbate mood swings.

🐦 Use uplifting essential oils such as lemon myrtle, ginger, and orange in your bath water, or in an infuser. For postnatal depression, jasmine, clary sage, and ylang-ylang are recommended. Mix them in equal parts and use just one drop in your bath water or infuser.

🐦 Homeopathic Nat. Mur is a classic remedy for PPD. Alternatively, the Bach flower remedies walnut, star of Bethlehem, mimulus, and rock rose can also give you a boost.

🐦 Keep a journal—a refuge for your up and down feelings.

🐦 Get some exercise—even if it's only a stroll in the sunshine on your earliest days as a mom, you'll get a boost from the fresh air, sun, and endorphins, the feel-good chemicals we produce when we exercise.

A brisk walk is a great mood lifter, releasing natural feel-good chemicals called endorphins.

Legumes such as lentils supply B vitamins which help lift your mood.

MORE THAN BLUES?

🐦 You feel permanently tired and lethargic.

🐦 You can't be bothered to bathe, dress properly, or care for your appearance.

🐦 You're anxious—worrying unjustifiably about the baby or other family members.

🐦 You can't sleep.

🐦 You can't cope with visitors.

The day .... *was born!*

Use this page to record your labor and birth.

Welcome baby!

Date

Time

Baby's weight

Baby's length

First feeding

Our first picture

Baby's First Year

So much has happened in the last nine months, but there will be so much more to record over the next year as your baby finds his place in the world—learning how to use his body and his voice to make his needs known and met! Use the pockets on this page to store special photos and a copy of your birth announcement card, together with any other mementos from the start of this precious new life.

Baby Firsts

Use these pages to jot down your memories about special "firsts" in your baby's life.

First smile

....

....

....

....

First cry

....

....

....

....

First looked in my eyes

....

....

....

....

First cuddle

....

....

....

....

First feeding

_____

_____

_____

First diaper change

_____

_____

_____

First visitors

_____

_____

_____

First journey

_____

_____

_____

First gifts

_____

_____

_____

_____

_____

Home At Last

Even if you gave birth to your baby at home, you may feel that same sense of being "back home at last" when the dust has settled and you're able to embark on your new routine.

During these early weeks, your own well-being is as important as your baby's. Be sure to get plenty of rest, and eat well—especially if you are breastfeeding.

Body matters

Your body may still look distressingly pregnant for the first few weeks, but don't be too worried about it—you'll soon be out of your maternity clothes, and you won't need to (and would be very unwise to) crash diet. In fact, if you're breastfeeding you need 500 more calories a day than you did pre-pregnancy—but make sure every calorie counts, packing in fruit, vegetables, whole grains, and pulses, and leaving out the empty calories such as candies, cookies, and chips. If you have a lot of fat stores left over from pregnancy (i.e. you used it as an excuse to overindulge!), you can afford to take fewer calories because your body will burn off the fat to produce milk. But the recommended additional 500 calories assumes you have some excess fat—so, if you're super skinny, you may need to eat even more than this.

In the early days you may be reluctant to put your baby down— cuddling him is a wonderful novelty.

Lowfat dairy products such as skim milk and cottage cheese provide the calcium you need for breastfeeding.

YOUR BREASTFEEDING DIET

🍃 Follow the healthy eating guidelines earlier in this book.

🍃 Have five calcium portions a day, and three portions of protein.

🍃 Drink at least eight glasses of fluids—more if it's hot and you're perspiring a lot—but don't overdo it, because excessive fluids can actually slow down your milk production.

Bonding

In the past, mothers were encouraged to establish a strict routine with their newborn babies from the earliest days, and cuddle time was restricted to just 10 minutes a day. But this is a time when you and your baby belong together. Instead of leaving him alone sleeping in an upstairs room, take him around the house with you in his crib or a sling so that you can see and hear him at all times and go to him when he cries. This will usually be because of hunger—and if you are nearby, he won't be kept waiting! You won't spoil him by picking him up and devoting yourself to him; and by going to him whenever he needs you, you will help him to feel loved and secure. Think of every cuddle being a boost to his growing confidence!

At night, keep your baby by your bed (this is in accordance with current safety guidelines for babies), so you can easily take him into bed with you for feeds. Wait until he's too big for his crib, and beginning to sleep through most nights, before moving him into a crib in his own room.

DIAPER CHANGING

🐚 Until you are confident enough to change your baby on your lap, use a changing mat or folded towel on a table or your bed—but make sure he can't roll off.

🐚 Have all his diaper-changing things ready and make sure the room is warm before you undress him.

🐚 Always wipe a girl from the front toward the anus. A good wash with plenty of water is the best way to remove every trace of feces and urine.

🐚 Gently dry the baby's buttocks and thighs well, paying attention to all the folds, before putting on the clean diaper.

🐚 If your baby's bottom seems red, it could be due to irritation from urine and feces—a baby's skin is very delicate. Frequent changes and extra care with cleansing can help. Natural calendula creams are good for soothing a sore bottom, but it also helps to let the baby kick without a diaper on to let the air reach his skin.

🐚 If his bottom looks really sore, and the baby's diaper smells of ammonia, get some help from your doctor or nurse—diaper rash can be very painful and will make your baby unhappy.

Diaper-changing time is another opportunity for you and other family members to communicate with your baby.

Six Weeks On

By the time your baby is six weeks old, you should be getting used to your new life as a mother. Physically, everything should be returning to normal too.

Your postpartum checkup

At your postpartum checkup, your doctor or midwife will want to know:

🐦 Is your weight on target?

🐦 Are your kidneys working properly? You may be asked to provide a urine sample for testing.

🐦 Is your blood pressure normal?

🐦 Have your stitches healed? If you still have any discomfort, tell your doctor.

🐦 Is your womb back to its pre-pregnant size?

🐦 Are you still bleeding? Do you have any vaginal discharge?

🐦 How are you feeling? If you're very tired, low or depressed, discuss this with your doctor.

Your baby's six-week checkup

At your baby's six-week checkup, the doctor will want to know the following:

🐦 How well is he feeding?

🐦 Does he have a sleep routine?

🐦 Is he beginning to support his head?

🐦 Does his heart sound healthy? The doctor will listen to it at this checkup.

🐦 Can the baby follow an object with his eyes?

🐦 Does he react to noises?

🐦 Does his hip joint fit properly into its socket?

The six-week checkup is a big event for your baby. You may be anxious, but that's normal.

NEWBORN HEARING TESTS

🐦 Ninety percent of newborn babies in the U.S. are now given a hearing screening—usually in the hospital a day or two after birth. The screen uses two simple tests which are painless for the baby. The Otacoustic Emissions test (OAE) involves a small earpiece, containing a speaker and microphone, being placed in the baby's ear. A clicking sound is played and if the cochlea is functioning properly, the earpiece will pick up an echo. The Automated Auditory Brainstem Response test (AABR) records brain activity in response to sounds. A series of clicking sounds is played through headphones over the baby's ears and small sensors on the baby's head pick up brain activity, which is displayed on a computer screen.

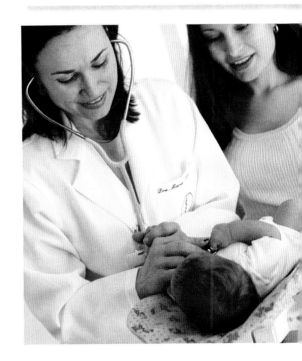

YOUR BODY NOW

🐚 After your six-week checkup—and with your midwife's or doctor's go-ahead—you can resume a more active life: walking, swimming, jogging, aerobics, cycling, and so on. You are also able to resume a normal sex life—and can do so even before your six-week checkup, although it's best to wait at least four weeks after having your baby. Lowered hormone levels can leave the vagina dry, so you may want to use a lubricating cream or jelly. Try different positions—side to side or woman on top give you more control, and put less pressure on your scar if you've had a tear or episiotomy.

You may be eager to get back into shape, but nervous about leaving your baby while you do so.

six weeks your baby feels established in his new world and may settling into a feeding and sleeping routine.

NOW WE ARE SIX (WEEKS)

From about a month old:

🐚 Your baby can press his feet down when held standing, and make reflex walking movements, but his arms are more active than his legs.

🐚 His pupils react to light and he can follow a moving object about 6-10 inches (15-25 cm) away from him. He gazes at your face intently when you feed him or talk to him. His alertness is growing all the time.

🐚 He's startled by sudden noises, but sleeps through most normal household sounds.

🐚 He cries loudly when he's hungry or uncomfortable, and makes little grunts when he's content.

🐚 He coos and chirrups when he's talked to, and grasps your finger when you touch his palm. He is learning all the time that he's awake—so use the time to talk, sing, and play with squeaky toys with him.

Back in Shape

Pilates and yoga, non-jarring exercises that stretch and strengthen your body, will help you get your figure back. They'll also improve your posture and relieve the strain on your shoulders of constantly lifting and carrying your baby. Try the following:

TUMMY TONERS

1 Lie on your back with your knees bent, feet hip-width apart. Rest your arms on your tummy. Keep your pelvis neutral, so it's not tilting forward or backward. If you had a bowl of water resting on it, there would be no risk of it spilling. Breathe in, and, as you breathe out, soften the front of your pelvis, enabling your belly button and lower abdominal muscles to pull down toward your spine. Imagine you're lying in a hammock and hold your abdominals in this hollow position, feeling your spine lengthen. On your next in-breath, relax your muscles again. Repeat five times.

2 Starting in the same position as the last exercise, breathe in, and then, as you breathe out, hollow your lower abdominals, drawing your belly button back to the spine and lengthening your tailbone away—but keeping it on the floor. Still breathing out, slide your right leg away on the floor and take your right arm above your head to touch the floor behind. Stretch from your fingertips to your toes, without allowing your back to arch. Breathe in as you return your arm and leg to the starting position. Repeat the exercise five times on each side.

EASY DOES IT

❧ Ease yourself back into an exercise routine slowly. This is especially important if you've had a Cesarean, or if you are suffering with a lot of backache. A specialized postnatal exercise class will help with this—and your teacher will also be able to address your individual problems. Sometimes very subtle adjustments to your exercise program can make the difference between pain and gain—you just need to be shown the correct method!

Very young mothers seem to get back into shape with minimal effort, but when we are older, we have to work much harder.

xercises that stretch and strengthen your
ody will help you to get your figure back.

OTTOM FIRMER

ie on your right side in a straight line with your arm
tretched out and your head resting on it. Bend your
ght leg in front of you at the knee. Use your left arm to
upport you, and keep lifting your waist off the floor while
aintaining the length in your trunk. Raise your left leg so
at it's in line with your hips, about 6 inches (15 cm) off
e floor. Rotate your leg slightly from the hip and flex your
ot toward your face. Breathe out as you slowly lift your leg
out 7 inches (18 cm), then breathe in and lower it. Raise
d lower the same leg ten times without touching the floor
between, breathing out as you raise it and in as you lower
Then turn over and repeat on the other side.

PPER BODY STRESS RELIEVER

e on your back with your knees bent and feet hip-width
art, flat on the floor. Keep your neck long, using a small
t pillow if this helps. Raise both arms up to the ceiling,
owing your shoulder blade to come off the floor. Reach
rough to your fingertips, stretching your arm as
 as it will go. Breathe out as you let your whole
oulder release down to the floor. Repeat with
e other arm, then repeat ten times with each
m alternately.

BEST POSTNATAL EXERCISE

PILATES Try floor exercises that use the
abdomen as a strong anchor from which the rest of
the body can be safely stretched and strengthened.
The exercises can help a range of problems and will
also improve your posture and give you narrower
hips, trimmer thighs, and stronger abdominal and
back muscles. They're highly recommended if you've
had back problems following pregnancy.

YOGA Stretching postures can strengthen and
tone the body as well as making it more supple and
flexible—useful when you're handling a baby. Yoga
helps the inner organs work more efficiently, aiding
digestion and circulation, and giving you a general
feeling of well-being.

METHOD PUTKISTO A method of stretching,
developed with the help of a chiropractor and sports
doctor, that helps you get into positions you thought
only Olympic gymnasts could manage. Method
Putkisto lengthens the muscles and gives space to
inner organs which become squashed and restricted
by poor posture.

Don't exercise too vigorously,
particularly if you have had a Cesarean
section. Seek specialized advice on
postnatal exercise so that you get the
most out of your fitness routine.

Your Baby at 0-3 Months

Make the most of these precious weeks, during which time you and your partner will get to know your baby and adjust to life as new parents.

WEEKS 1-2

Your baby is awake only ten percent of the time. When he is awake, he may be looking around quietly ("quiet alert") and gradually focusing on your face. From your point of view, this is a great time to bond as you notice him take in a little bit more of your face every day.

WEEKS 3-4

He now jumps at loud noises and is even starting to lift and hold his head off the floor.

WEEK 5

When you squeak a toy, or ring a little bell, he will turn his head toward the sound.

WEEK 6

You may notice him making sounds with more than one syllable. His first words! Start playing with him more, taking your lead from him. If he seems uninterested, he may not be in the mood. Try again later.

WEEK 7

He could be starting to roll over at this age, and, when you clap, he may try to copy you.

WEEK 8

He's getting better at focusing on smaller objects, such as buttons. Encourage this skill, but don't put anything tiny within his reach—he will soon be able to grasp small objects, which could be a choking hazard.

WEEK 9

Your baby may now be laughing out loud when you tickle him and talk to him, and squealing with delight when he sees you.

WEEK 10

He may already be able to shake a rattle and laugh at the sound he creates.

WEEKS 11-12

When he hears you talk, he'll turn to see you. When you pull him up to a sitting position, he may be able to hold his head in line with the rest of his body; and, when you pull him to a standing position, he may start putting some weight on his legs—though he's not steady yet.

A young baby learns new skills every day and begins to interact with the world around him.

CRADLE CAP (BABY DANDRUFF)

🐦 Cradle cap is harmless but unsightly, causing the scalp to look scaly with skin that falls off in flakes. You can rub the baby's scalp with olive oil, which should then be left on for two hours before being rubbed vigorously with a rough, dry towel. Shampoo the excess oil off at bath time.

Sticky eye

This is another common problem for babies, which should be treated as soon as you first notice any discharge. Make up some salt water solution, using a level teaspoon of salt in 1 pint/568 ml of cooled, boiled water, and wipe the eye with this, using a cotton wool ball. Some mothers have also found that wiping the affected eye with breast milk can improve sticky eyes.

When babies seem inconsolable most evenings, but they are otherwise thriving and healthy, they are said to have "colic."

How tiny are you?

Use this space for a hand or a foot print from your baby.

Cry baby!

How long should a baby cry for? Research in the 1980s found that the average baby cries for two hours a day at six weeks old—although one in four continued for over three hours. The good news is that, by three months old, most cried for no more than an hour a day.

If your baby starts crying inconsolably and continues for hours at a time, he could have colic. Check first that he doesn't need changing, feeding, or burping, and that he doesn't have a temperature, a rash, or any other sign of illness. Picking him up and carrying him on your shoulder may comfort him and ease any tummy pain (from trapped wind), and a weak fennel infusion, sweetened with honey, can also help (give it three or four times a day).

Your Baby's Routine in the First 3 Months

If you are a creature of habit—if your life revolves around regular meal times and sleep patterns—then it's natural to hope that your baby will not choose a routine that throws your own into disarray. But whether to actively establish a routine for your baby, or to just go with the flow, is a huge area of contention.

Babies like routine—it makes them feel happy and secure; and, left to their own devices, they will fall into a routine that you can use to your advantage. For example, you will soon discover how long your baby likes to sleep after a feeding, and how long after a sleep he will need feeding again. You can help things along with little routines of your own, such as always doing things in a particular order—a bath before bedtime, for example, and songs and games after a diaper change.

ROUTINE PROS AND CONS

Some parents love baby routines, others loathe them. Think hard about what will best suit you.

PROS

🐦 You have structure to your day, and a sense of control.

🐦 Babies are happier and thrive better when they know what's coming next—even at this early age.

🐦 If your baby's in bed early, you have more time to spend with your partner.

🐦 If the routine works, you may even be getting a full night's sleep by the time the baby is just six weeks old!

CONS

🐦 If you're breastfeeding, your baby will dictate the feeding pattern—so imposing a routine may be a struggle.

🐦 A routine makes your life inflexible—difficult if you have a lifestyle that involves leaving the house often, because you'll be confined to your home during your baby's rest times.

🐦 The early weeks of motherhood may seem difficult enough to cope with, without the added chore of timetabling your baby.

🐦 If it's hard to stick to, or your baby doesn't take to it, you risk feeling like a failure.

Tune into your baby's natural routine if you are not imposing a routine on him—find out what suits you best.

Baby routines were first popularized by the Dr Frederic Truby King Method in the 1950s.

When you allow your baby to dictate his own routine, you will leave him to nap for as long as he likes. If you hate the idea of waking a sleeping baby—and many childcare experts do—then going with the baby's routine may be best for you. It may mean, however—and especially in these early weeks—that your baby takes his naps at different times of day, day-to-day, or week-to-week; there is also the chance that your baby will get so much sleep during the day that he stays up most of the evening, when you might be ready and yearning for time out from him, to wind down as a couple.

If you think a more regimented approach might suit you better, there are several books on the market advocating strictly administered baby routines. It is claimed that such routines will get your baby sleeping through the night from an early age; that your baby will also be less likely to suffer from colic; and that he will still feed regularly and well from either breast or bottle. The thought of adopting a routine may seem a great idea if you are a routine kind of person. But, by the same token, if you are a creature of habit, do you really want someone else's routine imposed on you?

A DAILY ROUTINE FOR YOUR BABY

Babies reared on strict routines are up, changed, and fed by 7 am (but will you be, too?).
Here's how the day pans out for a six- to eight-week old who is breastfed:

🐾 Feedings at: 7 am, 10.45 am, 2/2.30 pm, 6.15 pm, 10.30 pm.

🐾 Nap times at: 9-9.45 am, 11.45-2 pm, 4.30-5 pm.

🐾 Bedtime is at 7 pm, but the baby is woken again at 10 or 10.30 pm for a late-night feeding that should persuade him to sleep through the night. Babies are woken from naps by being unswaddled and having the lights on so that they wake naturally. Night feedings should always be kept low-key—dim lights, minimal fuss, etc.—so that the baby recognizes that this is sleep time, not play time.

This is what we did

....

....

....

....

....

....

....

Your Baby at 3-6 Months

No two babies develop at exactly the same rate, but baby "milestones" have been noted with such accuracy that you can predict roughly what should happen and when. Here's what to expect in the first three to six months:

🐚 **3 MONTHS** By now your baby's body is completely uncurled and his legs are extended. His hands stay open though most babies can't grasp anything for long. Intellectually, your baby is showing signs of curiosity in the world around him—and particularly in you, and what you are doing!

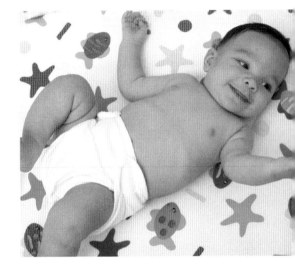

Give your baby the chance to kick his legs freely without the restriction of clothing.

CURING CRYING

Try the following:
🐚 Play classical music to your baby.
🐚 Take him for a walk in his stroller.
🐚 Have a skin-to-skin cuddle.
🐚 Sing lullabies.
🐚 Swaddling—keeping a baby wrapped up tight—reminds him of his comfy time in the womb.
🐚 Sucking on breast, bottle, or a dummy helps your baby relax.
🐚 Shushing—loud shushing noises, made either by you, or by a hairdryer or vacuum cleaner, are supposed to sound like the noise your baby heard in the womb—the whooshing of blood flowing through your arteries.

🐚 **4 MONTHS** Your baby can now roll from side to side and onto his back. He will also support himself on his forearms, and he's discovered his hands, which he sucks and plays with. Early speech is developing—he may make sound like "Ma" and "Pa," though he doesn't understand what he saying. Feeding times cause great excitement now, and he loves being propped up so he can have a good look around

🐚 **5 MONTHS** If you place your baby on his tummy, he will push his head well clear of the mattress and he can roll from his back onto his side. He's discovered his feet and likes sucking them—in fact, he looks like a regular yogi he's so flexible! At this age he's also starting to sense when things are different, strange, or scary, and he can express fear, disgust, and anger.

READY FOR SOLIDS?

Solid foods shouldn't normally be introduced before the age of six months, but the criteria for introducing "real food" are:

🐾 When your baby is double his birth weight (usually at six months).

🐾 When he can hold his head up and sit well when supported (e.g. propped by cushions in his high chair).

🐾 When he's able to cope with food being put in his mouth—too soon and he will reject it automatically. Babies are born with a reflex called "tongue thrust," which causes them to push things out of their mouths as a safeguard against choking. If your baby does this when you try to feed him, wait a while longer. He's not ready yet.

🐾 He doesn't seem satisfied by his milk feedings— e.g. he's waking up regularly during the night, demanding food.

🐾 He's started reaching out for your own food (although this is strictly off limits).

If you do decide to give your baby solids before six months, stick to baby rice, and puréed fruit and vegetables. Avoid wheat (including rusks), dairy products, citrus fruits and berries, nuts, fish, eggs, honey, salt, and sugar. These foods are the most likely to cause health problems or trigger allergies.

How you've grown

Use this space for a new foot or hand print—hasn't your baby grown!

🐾 **6 MONTHS** By six months, your baby can twist in all directions. He can probably sit unsupported, too, for a couple of seconds. He's able to hold an object between his finger and thumb, and may be able to rotate his wrist. If you show him his reflection in a mirror, he'll be delighted and intrigued. This is the age at which many babies are weaned, and he will already show a preference for certain foods.

If you think your baby is very hungry, ask your doctor if you should introduce solids before the age of six months.

Your Baby's Routine at 3-6 Months

Now that your baby is out of the newborn stage, you'll notice a few changes in him. Apart from the fact that he's physically more developed, his crying will have changed, and he now uses it to communicate with you. His cries start to mimic real language and he uses them, along with his expressive face, to tell you want he wants.

His sleep patterns are changing, too, and, even if you didn't impose a routine on him, he will probably have imposed one on himself—tending to nap at the same times of day in relation to his meals and playtimes. It is useful to observe his pattern and use it to your advantage—it means you know roughly when, and for how long, you will be able to get on with other things—and there always seems to be a huge amount to do when a small baby is in the house! If you're using non-disposable diapers, there's the laundry to

TYPICAL ROUTINE

Routines change very subtly for your baby as he grows up.

❧ At 3-6 months a typical routine will include feedings at 7 am, 11 am, 2.15/2.30 pm, 6.15 pm, 10.30 pm, and naps at 9-9.45 am and 12 noon-2/2.15 pm. Your baby is getting no more than three hours' sleep during the day (you're still encouraging him to wake up "naturally" by turning lights on, uncovering him, and bustling about in his room)—and this encourages him to sleep longer at night. The routine also includes a bath at 6 pm followed by a massage before he's put into his pajamas. His 6.15 feeding is his bedtime meal, but he has some time to get used to the idea of bed, with the lights dimmed while he sits in his rocker and you quietly tidy up around him for about ten minutes. Then it's off to bed at 7 pm—in the dark, with the door shut. The late-night feeding is just to keep him going so that he doesn't wake up hungry during the night.

Your baby's nap time is an opportunity for you to catch up on other things.

get on with; and, if you're bottle feeding, the whole process of washing bottles and then making up fresh ones is enormously time-consuming—and not something that can be put off. You have to do it every day.

However, exactly how much time you will have for all the things you have to do is impossible to predict. Studies show that even from birth, individual needs for sleep vary enormously. But by three or four months, your baby should be ready for more spacious quarters in a dropside crib, and, if he's no longer waking for night feedings, you can move him into a room of his own—as long as you will still be able to hear him at night if he does wake and cry. Use his room for his naps, too.

Early evening is often a bad time for new moms, tired from looking after the baby all day—and babies tend to become slightly frenzied at this time, too. The fact that you are inadvertently hurrying his feeding or rushing through diaper time to get on with making dinner may aggravate him more; and, in turn, you will get even more het up. If you've been able to establish a routine, and your baby is sticking to it, this may offset some of the tension to which you are both susceptible. If your baby is the type to scream inconsolably

Your baby will love being part of your multitasking world! Keeping your baby close to you will strengthen the bonding process.

all evening, you may have to accept that everything else must go on hold while you sit holding him—or you may decide to tweak your own schedule, using this time to take him for an early evening walk with the dog or put him in his car seat to drive somewhere (try to fit it in with something you need to do, so you both benefit).

If your partner is around to help you, make the most of it—and let him bath the baby or give him a feeding. Your baby will probably be as glad to see a fresh face as you will be to hand him over to a willing pair of arms.

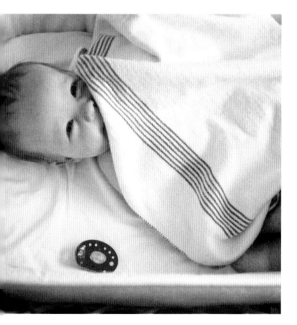

Always put your baby down to sleep on his back to reduce the risk of crib death.

Your Baby at 6-9 Months

At six months old your baby comes into his own. This is the recommended time to introduce solids—real foods—into his diet, which also enables him to take a more active part in family life, sitting in his own high chair at the table. Even if he needs a few cushions around him at first, he will soon be holding his own body unsupported while sitting, and he's also getting ready to crawl—supporting the top half of his body on outstretched arms and bending his knees up. If he doesn't crawl, instead developing a kind of shuffle (on his bottom, or using one leg under him to propel himself forward), that's fine—what matters is that he is making himself mobile. Once this happens, though, beware. He will quickly pick up speed,

SAFETY FIRST

🐦 Never leave the baby alone, unless he's sleeping in his crib.

🐦 Remove all furniture with sharp corners and edges from his reach.

🐦 Don't have wires trailing across the floor.

🐦 Cover all sockets with safety plugs.

🐦 Keep fires guarded.

🐦 Make sure cupboard doors can't be opened by your baby.

🐦 Know exactly what is within his reach at all times, and be sure it is entirely safe to him.

🐦 Consider having a playpen if you have the space. Some people hate the idea of these as they look like baby cages. Others find them invaluable—Your baby is safe in one place, with toys around him, while you get on with things nearby.

MILESTONES

SITTING UNSUPPORTED
🐦 When? 7-8 months.

CRAWLING
🐦 When? 6-9 months.

JUMPING AND DANCING WHEN YOU HOLD HIM UP STANDING
🐦 When? 6-8 months.

UNDERSTANDING WHEN YOU SAY "NO!"
🐦 When? 8 months.

BECOMING MORE WILFUL
🐦 When? 9 months.

USING EARLIEST WORDS—BEEBE, DADA, MAAMA
🐦 When? 7 months.

BABBLING AND SHOUTING
🐦 When? 8 months.

and needs to be watched. Encourage his curiosity, putting toys just out of his reach so he has a motive to go to them, but always think "safety first." Move anything fragile, along with pets' feeding bowls and rubbish bins. Keep anything he could swallow well out of reach, and check that furniture cannot be easily pulled over if he holds on to it.

Jeans or pants are good work-wear for your baby at this stage, as he's going to get much dirtier than before, and his knees will also take quite a bashing.

Babies are naturally inquisitive. Encourage your baby's curiosity within safe boundaries.

Look at you now!

Use this space for a photo of your baby.

WHAT'S NORMAL?

AT 6 MONTHS

- Passing toys from one hand to the other.
- Holding toys in one hand rather than two.
- Rolling in both directions.
- Cutting his first tooth.
- Blowing raspberries and making other funny noises.

AT 7 MONTHS

- Poking objects to make them move.
- Sitting unaided.
- Getting noisier all the time—banging and clapping objects.
- Blowing kisses.

AT 8 MONTHS

- Yanking and pulling—don't leave anything dangling (it could be hazardous).
- Crawling or shuffling.
- Clapping hands.
- Waving bye-bye.
- Picking up "finger foods."

AT 9 MONTHS

- Throwing food on the floor.
- Using furniture as a prop for standing up.
- Working out how to put one toy on top of another.

Your Baby's Routine at 6-9 Months

The physical milestones reached in this quarter of your baby's first year mean inevitable changes to the routine, too. As your baby starts to eat solids, you will want to introduce him to mealtimes that coincide with yours. Being given "real food" will have an impact on his energy levels, and it could cause him some digestive problems that have to be addressed. He's also starting to teethe, and becoming more active. All these new things in his life can make him a baby who's ready for a regular routine with plenty of sleep–but they can also cause him to become fretful, over-tired, uncomfortable, or overstimulated, all of which could interfere with his sleep patterns–and yours.

Don't let a routine squeeze out the fun from your baby's day–your baby will get pleasure from something as simple as rolling around.

If you're following a strictly scheduled routine, your baby will still be on roughly the same pattern as before–with feedings at 7 am, 11.45 am, 2.30 pm, 5 pm and 6.30 pm, and naps at 9-9.30/45 and 12.30-2.30 pm. If you're introducing solids, do so (starting with baby rice) after the 11.45 am feeding, and introduce new foods, and increasing amounts, every couple of days. Your baby should soon be having some food at lunchtime, and then some in the mid-afternoon or early evening. By seven months, he needs a protein food at lunchtime, as he will now have run out of the iron stores he was born with. The body is actually capable of digesting protein from six months, so, if you ended up weaning earlier than this, six months is the time to start with protein.

Sticking to such a strict regime works for a lot of women, but it can make your own life seem unsustainable.

If mealtimes are fun and enjoyable, you will have more luck when introducing your baby to new foods.

Where are the spaces for your lunches out and visits to friends? Do you have to fit all your shopping and outdoor activities into the small gaps when your baby is awake, but not being fed or prepared for the next sleep?

Other factors you need to consider in relation to your baby's routine now include:

🐝 Breastfeeding—this may make it hard to keep to a routine. Seek help from a breastfeeding counselor.

🐝 Going back to work—if someone else will be looking after your baby, or your baby will be attending a day nursery, how will his routine fit in with his carer's?

🐝 How does your baby's routine fit in with that of his siblings if you have other children to consider?

🐝 If you're a stay-at-home mom, will you have to stay at home all the time? Will your baby's naps and feeding times give you the freedom to drop him off at child care while you take an exercise class or go for a swim?

🐝 If keeping to a routine is adding stress to your life, give it up! Your instinct is telling you it isn't right for you.

SLEEP PROBLEMS

If your baby hasn't fallen into a neat pattern of sleeping through the night, or has started waking a lot, your own sleep deprivation can quickly become an obsession and something you can end up feeling quite resentful about.

To cope:

🐝 Find a babysitter, so you can sleep during the day. Sleeping when your baby does sounds sensible but isn't always practical—besides, that's when you're busy making up the bottles, puréeing baby vegetables, and catching up on the laundry!

🐝 Avoid a junk food diet—it's tempting when your blood sugar levels are low and you want a quick pick-me-up, but slow release carbs like beans, wholewheat bread, and brown rice are better for sustaining your energy.

🐝 Go for a brisk walk—the fresh air will do you and your baby good, so make it a priority to get out every day, whatever the weather.

🐝 Introduce good sleep habits for your baby—a bedtime routine is a good start, even if you begin now with a bath followed by a last feeding, and a cuddle in a dimly lit room. Keep nap times consistent—keeping your baby up all day won't necessarily make him sleepier at night. He could get overtired and hysterical.

Make sure your baby's new careprovider is happy to do things the way you and your baby are used to.

Your Baby at 9-12 Months

Once your baby is on the move, so much more of the world becomes accessible to him—be vigilant and safety conscious!

Hard to believe that your baby has now been around for as long as you were pregnant! Already he is speeding through his baby milestones. By nine months old, he's making determined efforts to crawl (if he's not already doing so) and some, rare, babies are even on their feet and walking (though these are the ones most likely to have bumps and bruises, as their bodies are ahead of their brains!). His dexterity is improving all the time. He can use his forefinger to poke into holes—so if you haven't yet covered up the plug sockets, now's the time to do so. His balance is already so well developed that he can swing his torso round, and reach forward without wobbling over.

Ten months is the age at which he has good enough muscle control in his knees and feet to start pulling himself up on any nearby furniture and then cruise from chair to chair—always hanging on to something. Do take care that furniture he may reach for won't tumble on top of him. This stage can arrive very suddenly—and even inappropriately, for example when you're staying away from home in unfamiliar surroundings. Try to think one step ahead of your inquisitive baby.

To help him stand safely:

🌿 Don't put socks or bootees on his feet—they'll be too slippery.

🌿 Resist the temptation to help him along—babies are ready to walk in their own sweet time.

🌿 Don't play tricks such as removing your support—he'll lose trust in you and be frightened.

🌿 If you haven't previously used a sleeping bag for your baby, don't introduce one now. If he's trying to stand in his cot, he will topple and could hurt himself.

You funny thing!

....

....

....

....

....

WHAT'S NORMAL NOW?

AT 10 MONTHS
🐦 He's assertive, knows exactly what he wants, and how to let you know about it!
🐦 He can copy gestures and expressions.
🐦 He can roll a ball or drop it when you ask him to.
🐦 He can play alongside other children, though not actually with them.
🐦 He gets scared of loud noises.
🐦 He can understand when you say "no"—and may choose to ignore it!

AT 11 MONTHS
🐦 He can point his finger.
🐦 He can hand over toys—and snatch them back again.
🐦 He can try to feed himself with a spoon.
🐦 He may need lots of reassurance, and will keep coming back to you to "touch base."

AT 12 MONTHS
🐦 He may be starting to walk—but he may still be many months off this landmark. Both scenarios are normal.
🐦 He can gesture to get things he wants, pointing and repeating a sound (which may have nothing to do with the object) insistently.
🐦 He can perform simple actions in order, hold crayons, and put objects such as beakers inside each other; he can pick up small foods like peas between his finger and thumb, and when you ask him to point to his nose, he can do so.

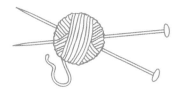

Your baby's speech is also becoming noticeably more elaborate at this age. Listen out for multi-syllable phrasing, such as "Babamamalala"—he's on his way to talking, and his first real word will come at around 10-11 months. Usually it's the name of someone important to him. Try not to be too disappointed if this happens to be the family cat or dog, rather than Mama!

Help your baby's speech
🐦 Use pronouns—say: "I'll get your coat" and "Here's your ball." He learns by labeling things, and you will be increasing his vocabulary every time you do so.
🐦 Don't be frustrated if he doesn't pronounce words properly—it won't help him to have you ask him to keep on trying to get a word right. Just accept that he hasn't got it yet, but will do eventually.

Make sure your baby feels safe and secure as he makes his first attempts at walking.

Your Baby's Routine at 9-12 months

We've met mothers who haven't thought about the word "routine" until way beyond their baby's first birthday—everything happens in a laid-back and organic way, which is fine when both of you are happy, well-fed, and getting enough sleep. But when things start to go wrong—"he's always hungry!"/"he's never hungry!"/"he's always fretful"/"I can't read him, I don't know what he wants!"/"he's still awake when we've gone to bed!"—you may need to seek help from a childcare expert, and the first thing that expert will want to know is, "What's his routine?"(or, indeed, "Does he have one?"). If your baby still doesn't have a routine, it's not too late to start now—although, for a baby who's not used to one at all, it may take some time and patience to settle him in. So be prepared to persevere if you want this to work.

Here's how a typical day might pan out—would this suit your lifestyle?

🐾 7-8 am: wake and get your baby up, change his diaper, and give him a drink of formula from a sippy cup (babies don't move on to cow's milk until after one year old) or, if you're still breastfeeding, give him an early morning feeding. This should be followed by breakfast—cereal mixed with formula or breast milk.

🐾 After breakfast: a wash before getting dressed, followed by time to play on a rug or in his playpen. Alternatively, your baby could have some toys on his high chair tray to keep him occupied while you busy around, providing extra entertainment if you don't have time to play.

Your baby is becoming more independent all the time—but he still needs to feel safe and secure at all times.

CONTROLLED CRYING

The "controlled crying" technique is supposed to help babies unlearn the bad sleep habits they've learned. The advice is to leave your baby to cry (in bed, when he's tired and you know he's really ready to sleep) for a set number of minutes before going to check on him and reassure him (without picking him up). Repeat the pattern at increasing intervals of time until he falls asleep. Start by going in after five minutes, then leave it a little longer, and longer. Some mothers can never bring themselves to put this technique into practice, as it breaks their hearts to think of their baby crying to be picked up. But we have come across children of six who cannot get to sleep without their mother lying next to them.

With the "controlled crying" technique, babies soon learn that someone will come to them before too long.

When your baby shows signs of tiredness—becoming fretful, for example—put him down for a morning nap, but many babies are cutting back on daytime sleeps by this age. If he's not used to being put down for a nap and starts to cry, most childcare experts think it's OK to let him cry for a short while—a technique known as "controlled crying."

Pre-lunch play—have some friends round for coffee and let the babies mix, or go for a walk.

Lunchtime—it's a good idea to start the meal with food rather than fluids, which will fill your baby up and stifle his appetite. After lunch, when you clear up, he can watch you from his chair with some toys on his tray.

If your baby has an afternoon nap as part of his routine, make it earlier rather than later, if you want him to go to bed early in the evening.

Afternoon activities could include a walk, playtime (see our ideas for games you can play with your baby on pages 126-7), and visits to friends.

Dinner, at around 5 pm, is another meal when he should have solids first and drinks later, but give him a good milk feeding before bed.

Always have a good bedtime routine that slows him down rather than speeds him up. If you do a lot of stimulating things before bedtime—listening to loud music, watching TV, working, and so on—it is harder to get to sleep than if you have a soporific bath with dimmed lights and soft music, then read quietly before turning out the light. Babies are the same!

Plot Your Baby's Growth

Use this chart to record your baby's weight over the first year.

	JANUARY	FEBRUARY	MARCH	APRIL	MAY	JUNE
4 lb 8 oz 2 kg						
5 lb 8 oz 2.5 kg						
6 lb 9 oz 3 kg						
7 lb 10 oz 3.5 kg						
8 lb 10 oz 4 kg						
9 lb 14 oz 4.5 kg						
11 lb 5 kg						
12 lb 5.5 kg						
13 lb 2 oz 6 kg						
14 lb 5 oz 6.5 kg						
15 lb 6 oz 7 kg						
16 lb 8 oz 7.5 kg						
17 lb 9 oz 8 kg						
18 lb 11 oz 8.5 kg						
20 lb 9 kg						
21 lb 9.5 kg						
22 lb 10 kg						
23 lb 2 oz 10.5 kg						
24 lb 4 oz 11 kg						
25 lb 5 oz 11.5 kg						
26 lb 7 oz 12 kg						
27 lb 8 oz 12.5 kg						
28 lb 10 oz 13 kg						

Plot Your Baby's Growth

	JULY	AUGUST	SEPTEMBER	OCTOBER	NOVEMBER	DECEMBER
lb 8 oz kg						
lb 8 oz .5 kg						
lb 9 oz kg						
lb 10 oz .5 kg						
lb 10 oz kg						
lb 14 oz .5 kg						
lb kg						
lb .5 kg						
lb 2 oz kg						
lb 5 oz .5 kg						
lb 6 oz kg						
lb 8 oz 5 kg						
lb 9 oz kg						
lb 11 oz 5 kg						
lb kg						
lb 5 kg						
lb kg						
lb 2 oz 5 kg						
lb 4 oz kg						
lb 5 oz 5 kg						
lb 7 oz kg						
lb 8 oz 5 kg						
lb 10 oz kg						

First Foods

The recommended age at which a baby should be introduced to solids is currently six months. This is because research shows that by this age a baby has developed protective bacteria to help his digestive system tolerate new foods. Occasionally, experts will recommend that very hungry babies are given solids earlier—seek advice if your baby still seems hungry after his usual milk feedings, and is waking up hungry in the night, having previously slept right through.

Even though you are introducing solids, his milk feeding remains his most important source of nutrition in the early weeks, and the food is an added bonus. His first solid meal is just a teaspoon or so of baby rice, mixed with your baby's usual milk (formula or breast) until it's the consistency of yogurt, and served on a baby spoon.

Once you have established that he's happy with the baby rice (try it over several days, and see if you can

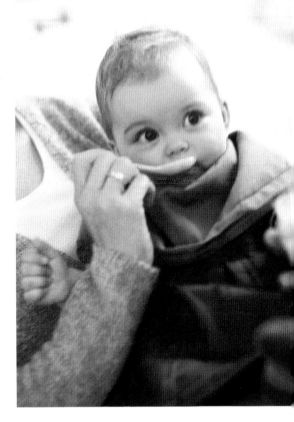

Your baby is ready for weaning at six months, and you may be surprised how quickly your baby takes to his new diet.

You can purée a range of foods—colorful vegetables are a great starter food for babies.

GETTING STARTED

YOU WILL NEED:

- A blender to purée food.
- A strainer to get rid of lumps.
- A small plastic bowl—preferably with a lid, so you can store food you have prepared.
- A shallow, plastic baby spoon. These are easy to sterilize and comfy for your baby's mouth. Spoons that show if food is too hot (by changing color) are also very useful.
- Bibs to protect your baby's clothes.
- An ice cube tray for freezing small portions of puréed food, or special containers with lids for freezing.

increase the amount he takes), you can introduce some other foods—puréed pear is a good one to start with. In the early days, offer it at a separate mealtime to the baby rice, and always give the breastfeed first.

When you introduce puréed vegetables (mix them with a little baby milk to get the consistency nice and runny, like yogurt), start with the naturally sweeter ones like carrots, butternut squash, and sweet potato. They will be more palatable to your baby than broccoli and spinach, which can be introduced later.

It's worth remembering that it takes about 12 attempts with a food for a baby to get used to its taste—so some of the more challenging ones may require quite a bit of perseverance on both your parts before your baby will accept them. If something is rejected one day, leave a few days before offering it again—and only offer a tiny amount at first, to test your baby's reaction.

Baby's favorite foods

....

....

....

....

....

....

....

....

....

SLOWLY DOES IT

🐤 Let your baby take the lead—rub a small amount of purée on his lips and let him lick it off. If he's happy with his first taste, give him a little more on the spoon.

🐤 Only put a small amount of food on the spoon, and only put the tip of the spoon in your baby's mouth—so he can decide how much he wants.

🐤 Never tip your baby back during a meal—he should be supported in an upright position at all times to avoid choking.

🐤 Watch out for any signs of a reaction to certain foods. Citrus fruits, strawberries, tomatoes, wheat, and fish should not be introduced until after your baby is nine months old, as they are common foods for triggering a reaction.

🐤 Don't add salt to his food, as it can put a strain on his kidneys.

🐤 Steer clear of sugar (including dried fruits), which can upset the balance of bacteria in your baby's gut, causing digestive problems.

🐤 Honey should also be avoided until after one year, as it contains a type of bacteria that produces toxins in a baby's intestines.

Mashed avocado is an excellent source of fatty acids that boost brain power. Give a small amount to your baby, and spice up the rest to make a delicious guacamole dip for the adults in your household!

Tricky Ingredients

Finger foods

Solids cannot be rushed, and your baby is not going to score any extra goals in the baby development Olympics for beating his best buddy to the finger food stage. However, neither is this a time for you to procrastinate. Once your baby has mastered the art of eating runny purées, and you have successfully been able to make them slightly lumpier without causing him to gag or throw his arms up in disgust, you can start moving on to so-called finger foods. This will probably be around eight months old, when you have also established a more formal breakfast, lunch, and dinner routine, and your baby will want to start feeding himself.

The idea of finger foods is that your baby can pick them up and experiment with them. Remember that all his apparent playing with the food—mushing it in his hands, and smearing it on his face, bib, and high chair tray—is helping him to develop physically and intellectually, so don't fret too much if it's not all going in his mouth as intended. In fact, you may be helping him to make friends with food, and develop a healthy appetite for it by stepping back (metaphorically) and resisting the temptation to force him to eat what's on his plate.

These finger foods will also help your baby learn to chew—an essential developmental step. Even though he doesn't have teeth yet, your baby can gum his way through finger foods, but always keep a close eye on him to make sure he doesn't choke;a and never let him eat while he's crawling or toddling around.

You may hate the idea of having food pasted all over your face, but your baby is unlikely to be fazed.

SAFETY TIPS

🐦 Wash all your baby's feeding equipment in hot water.

🐦 Don't feed straight from the jar, as the food will soon be contaminated and can't be used again.

🐦 Wash and peel all fruit.

🐦 Test cooked foods on your bottom lip to make sure they won't burn your baby.

GOOD FINGER FOODS INCLUDE:

- Baby breadsticks or rice cakes (make sure they are unsalted).
- Chopped up pasta.
- Fingers of bread.
- Meat (your baby is now old enough to cope with iron, and in fact he needs it now, too).
- Well cooked eggs—scrambled, or fingers of omelet.
- Fruit—banana and pear slices.
- Cooked chopped vegetables—if you normally enjoy broccoli and carrots "al dente," make them a bit softer for your baby so he can bite them with his gums. Once he's mastered these, gradually cook them more lightly so he gets the full benefit of the nutrients in them.

If you're short of time and far from the store, jars may offer a more varied diet than you can provide on a daily basis.

alongside finger foods, continue to offer some puréed foods—lean meat or poultry, lentils, mashed potatoes, and rice. Even though your baby is moving on to solids, he still needs his milk, too—regular breastfeeding or around pint/568 ml of formula a day. He can also have cooled, boiled water in a sippy cup with a spout. Resist pressure give your baby juice, or at least dilute it right down.

BABY JARS

Home-cooked food is the best and most nutritious for your baby, but it is also time-consuming. If you find jars are better suited to your lifestyle, there are some very good ones available that will introduce your baby to a range of new tastes and textures—even if those tastes are not quite as natural as they should be. Be reassured that all prepared baby food is governed by strict directives that limit salt, sugar, and other additives. A few years ago, there was a baby food scare when a potentially harmful chemical called semicarbazide (SEM) was found in the lids of some jars. The risk of your baby becoming ill is tiny, but, if you're concerned, simply throw away the top spoonful of food—if any of it is going to contain the stray chemical, it will be this top portion. There are alternatives to jars, too—frozen, canned, and dried foods. Whatever type of package you go for, stick to the storage and preparation directions printed on it.

Learning To Use a Spoon

If all is going according to plan, your baby should be starting to look forward to meals that include solids. It's so much fun for him that the question of when to offer him a spoon of his own is unlikely to arise. If you've been feeding him with a spoon alongside his attempts at feeding himelf with finger foods, he will simply grab the spoon from you! Let him experiment, and be prepared for plenty of mess—it's a good idea to spread out old newspaper under his high chair. Resist the urge to wipe every spill off his face. Wouldn't that drive you mad, if someone did it to you?

Using his own spoon is a huge step forward in your baby's development, so encourage all his attempts to do so. This is an act that helps his manual dexterity as well as speeding up his hand and eye coordination more than just about anything else he does. It will take several months for him to become a proficient spoon user, so until he's accomplished at it make sure you have a collection of clean spoons to hand so you can replace the ones he drops—and keep one for yourself, too, to help him along. If he's having trouble scooping up his food, you can hand him the shovel, train, or plane fully loaded!

HAPPY EATERS

Your baby's mealtimes are a happier experience if you are not tense.

Minimize the stress to yourself by keeping meals simple, so you don't feel resentful about the time you've put into preparing something that's ultimately fed to the floor.

Even if you're worried that your baby isn't taking enough food, he probably is. Discuss any genuine concerns with your pediatrician—they're experts at helping moms with fussy-eating babies—but bear in mind that a child will always eat if he's hungry, and his appetite may already be sated by his milk feedings.

Don't panic over the little your baby has eaten in one day—try to think about the week as a whole, and make sure that it's well balanced nutritionally over seven days.

Don't load his plate—his food will be more tempting if you keep to "nouvelle cuisine"-style portions with lots of color.

If he tries to get out of the chair during feeding, he's had enough. Don't put up a fight—he will come to associate mealtimes with unhappiness and feeding will become more of a problem for you.

It takes months for your baby to become adept at using a spoon.

D.I.Y. BABY MEALS
(FROM 9 MONTHS)

VEGETABLE & PASTA CHEESE (4-6 portions)

🐦 Steam 4 small broccoli florets and 4 cauliflower florets for 8 to 10 minutes, until tender. Cook a scant 1 cup of small penne or farfalle pasta according to the instructions on the package, or until tender, then drain.

Meanwhile, make the cheese sauce. Melt 1 1/2 tablespoons of sweet butter in a small, heavy-bottomed pan over a low heat. Gradually add 1 tablespoon of all-purpose flour, beating well to form a smooth paste. Cook for 30 seconds, stirring continuously. Add 3/4 cup of whole milk, a little at a time, whisking well to prevent any lumps from forming, then stir in 1/2 teaspoon of dried oregano. Simmer for 2 minutes until smooth and creamy, then mix in 1/2 cup of grated Cheddar cheese. Add the cooked cauliflower, broccoli, and pasta to the sauce and stir well. Finely chop or mash the mixture.

APPLE & PLUM YOGURT (2 portions)

🐦 Peel, core, and chop a small dessert apple, then place in a pan with 2 pitted ripe plums and 2 tablespoons of water. Bring to a boil, then reduce the heat and let simmer, covered, for 5 minutes, or until tender. Remove the plum skins and purée the fruit in a blender or press through a strainer until smooth. Mix the fruit purée with 4 to 6 tablespoons of plain yogurt, then serve.

Don't panic about the amount of food that is wasted—your baby won't let himself go hungry.

FOOD INTOLERANCES

🐦 Five percent of children are allergic to or intolerant of certain foodstuffs and the effects can be catastrophic—projectile vomiting, stomach pains, delayed growth, or anaphylactic shock (which can be fatal and needs urgent medical attention at the first signs—puffing of the lips, eyes, and tongue, quickly followed by breathing problems). The good news is that 90 percent of children grow out of their allergies. Always introduce new foods one at a time so you can check for any sinister reactions. The worst culprits are milk, eggs, and nuts.

Playing With Your Baby

Some new mothers are complete naturals when it comes to cooing and playing with their babies. Others of us find it harder—perhaps because we have little experience of babies before our own is born, or because we feel self-conscious and unsure of ourselves. If that sounds like you, here are a few tips to get you going.

Early days

There's no need for anything too sophisticated just yet. All you need to do now, play-wise, is to look your baby straight in the face. One of the first things that a baby responds to is the human face. Bring your face up close to his—less than 12 inches/30 cm—and make it as interesting as you can. Talk expressively so that your eyebrows move up and down, and your mouth opens into an "O." Move your head and, most important of all, smile! Look deep into your baby's eyes, making constant eye contact. This is the foundation of your relationship with your baby and will elicit the earliest responses that will make playing with him fun for him and rewarding for you, too. As the weeks go by, your baby will start to smile back, and attempt to mimic your expressions.

Two months

As babies don't see pale colors at this age, use bold black-and-white images to grab his attention. There's no pressure to educate your child—all sounds and sights are new and stimulating right now—you are just helping things along by providing something he can easily focus on. Try holding a brightly colored teddy above his head, give him a few seconds to focus on it, and then watch him follow it with his eyes as you move it slowly from side to side.

Three months

Entertain him. Babies love it when Mom sings nursery rhymes or dances—even if it's goofy and out of tune. You can start reading him repetitive little stories now, too, and incorporate them into his bedtime routine. By now he focuses instantly on the toys you hold up for him, so make them more fun with some funny voices or squeaks.

Five months

Invest in a door bouncer—it's a great way to encourage him to feel his toes on the floor, but don't let his legs bear too much weight. Don't leave him dangling and feeling abandoned by you, but use his door bouncer time to clap, laugh, and sing with him.

Six months

Start playing peekaboo—this is the age when babies realize that things disappear when they cover their eyes with their hands, but come back when they uncover them. You can either hide behind your own hands, or use one of the baby's

A securely fastened door bouncer provides plenty of fun for your baby if you are close at hand.

cheesecloths over his head. Make dressing time more fun by playing peekaboo as his vest or jumper goes over his head. Your baby will soon learn to initiate the game.

Seven months

Play games that encourage crawling. Pop him on his front to play for a while on his mat—when he's starting to raise his body, you can even crawl around yourself to encourage him.

Eight months

Introduce a few nursery rhymes with actions, and get out saucepans and wooden spoons that you can bang together to make noises (and help his hand-to-eye coordination).

Ten to twelve months

Take your baby to a singing class or baby gym where more play activities will be introduced. Look at picture books with him, pointing to the images and lingering on a page for as long as your baby is interested. Keep on talking, giving your baby a running commentary on the everyday world. Babies particularly love having animals pointed out to them, and by 12 months they should understand around 50 words.

e-to-eye contact and plenty of laughter are great ways to tablish close bonds and enjoy quality time with your baby.

Healthy Baby

In your baby's first few months it's a good idea to take advantage of your pediatrician baby clinic, where your baby will be weighed and measured and you can discuss any worries about feeding and development. Especially when you're new to motherhood, it's reassuring to know that everything is happening as it should. You will also be offered vaccinations for your baby, and these are another opportunity to meet with the nurse or doctor (whichever health professional takes this service in your area) and discuss any worries.

Doctor's visits don't have to be daunting—make them happy events now, to avoid tears in later years.

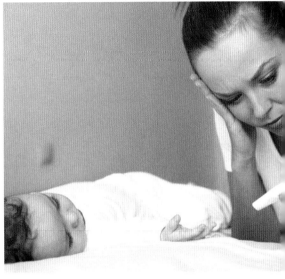

A baby's high temperature must always be taken seriously—seek medical advice for any baby under a year old who has a fever.

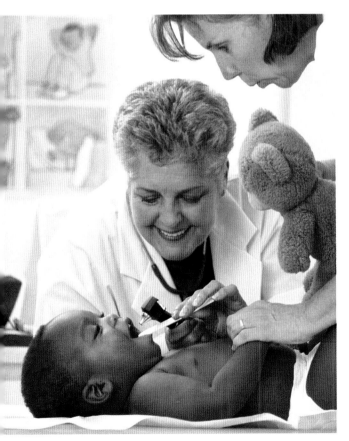

All babies develop at their own pace, but severe delays in reaching certain milestones can be cause for concern. Seek reassurance or advice (from your pediatrician initially) if:

- Your baby still can't support his head when you pick him up, or reach out for toys, after four to five months.
- He can't sit up, even when propped up, by six to seven months.
- Put any weight on his legs or sit independently by eight to nine months.
- Your baby is generally healthy but seems to have feeding problems.

Your pediatrician can help with breastfeeding problems (getting started, maintaining it, and finally stopping) and moving your baby on from a bottle to a cup. She's also the person to turn to for advice on problems such as cradle cap, colic, eczema, teething issues, and diaper rash.

If you're in doubt about your baby's health, and feel he s in any way unwell (and especially if he has a temperature bove 100.4ºF/38ºC, is vomiting, or has diarrhea), it is your octor you should turn to. And you should seek emergency edical advice in any of the following situations:

- Your baby is choking or struggling to breathe.
- He has a rash that won't disappear with pressure, or a tiff neck.
- He is suffering a fit.
- He has swallowed a hazardous household substance.
- He's showing signs of anaphylaxis—swelling face, lips, r eyes, and wheezy breathing.

Mother's instinct

Trust your gut feeling—you know your baby better than nyone else—and if you think there is something wrong with our baby, there probably is. If you think you may need edical help, phone your doctor. Friends and relatives may ry to reassure you but you are the one who knows that our baby is crying differently or being more subdued an usual.

IF YOUR BABY IS CHOKING

- Call for help (911).
- Stay calm. Don't attempt to dislodge the object by placing your fingers in the baby's mouth, as you could push it farther down.
- Lay the baby face down on your forearm or lap so his head and neck are supported and his head is lower than his body.
- Slap his back sharply with the palm of your hand—the object may fly out of his mouth. If it doesn't, turn him over to check in his mouth and only pick the obstruction out if it's now in the front of the mouth.
- If you haven't dislodged the obstruction after five attempts, turn him on his back and use the tips of two fingers to give him five chest compressions by pushing his breastbone downward and forward toward his face. Repeat these dislodging tactics up to three times while you wait for help to arrive.
- If your baby falls unconscious, try to rouse him by tapping his foot or calling his name. Lie him flat on his back and gently tilt his head back with one hand on his forehead. Check that he is breathing by watching his chest or putting your ear next to his face; hold him in your arms, with his head lower than his body, until the ambulance arrives.
- If he is not breathing, get telephone advice on how to give CPR—give details of any visible obstruction that is still there.

Your natural instinct means you should be able to recognize when your baby is unwell and needs medical help.

When Baby's Not Well

Even if it's just his first cold, your baby's first illness can be extremely upsetting. Recognizing the signs early on, and having some idea of what you can do, is empowering. It's a good idea to arm yourself with a baby health book, and pick up any leaflets you can from your baby clinic on dealing with commonplace problems. The list below is far from comprehensive, but will get you started.

COMMON COLD This causes a runny nose and tickly throat. The tickly throat can cause coughing, which in turn leads to vomiting, and this can be distressing for you and your baby. Prop up the baby's mattress so he is on a slight

Try to calm a baby who is in distress by talking soothingly to him—he will be reassured by the sound of your voice.

gradient, and the mucus can drain back instead of triggering a cough. A cold should start getting better rather than worse after five days. If it seems to be worsening, or he has other symptoms (at any point) such as swollen glands or difficulty keeping food and drink down, contact your doctor.

CONSTIPATION If your baby is struggling to open his bowels, or is producing dry, hard stools, make sure his diet is rich in fresh fruit and vegetables (if he's on solids) and that he's getting regular small sips of water. Call your doctor if your baby is very distressed, gets constipated often, or has blood in his diaper.

DIARRHEA AND VOMITING are signs of gastroenteritis, and babies can deteriorate rapidly because

they are quick to dehydrate. Ask your pharmacist for rehydration salts to replace the lost minerals quickly, and seek medical advice about what to give your baby to eat.

🐟 **FEVER** A baby temperature over 100.4°F/38°C is a fever, and a reaction to illness. It's the body's way of fighting infection, as the bugs causing the infection cannot live much above normal body temperature. Seek medical advice for any baby under a year who has a fever (and urgently when the baby is under six weeks), and try to get the temperature down by cooling your baby. Take his clothes off and leave him in his diaper. Cover him in bed with a sheet but not blankets. Give him plenty of cold drinks. Use a fan to cool his room, and wipe his forehead with a tepid cloth.

🐟 **RASH** Check out any rash, especially if accompanied by any form of malaise. A septicemic rash—one which accompanies meningitis and doesn't disappear when a tumbler is pressed to it—will only appear as a late symptom, so beware of earlier symptoms such as pallor, fever, and vomiting, a stiff neck, high pitched crying, and dislike of bright light. Seek urgent medical advice when any combination of these symptoms occurs. Chicken pox and measles (currently on the rise again) also cause a rash and the latter is a notifiable disease. If your health practice has a leaflet on baby rashes, grab a copy and keep it in your medical box for speedy reference.

KNOW YOUR BABY

Other signs that your baby is unwell include:

🐟 A usually active child moping and becoming uninterested in his toys.
🐟 A child who previously slept and ate well but is now constantly irritable.
🐟 Constant crying.
🐟 Dry diapers for over 9-12 hours.

BABY PAINKILLERS

🐟 Baby acetaminophen (Tylenol) can be used on babies over three months and is an excellent way of bringing down a temperature, working within 30-45 minutes. If your baby is younger than this, seek advice from your doctor first. Ibuprofen is also available in a baby dose, but is not suitable for children with asthma. Aspirin is not recommended for babies. Be sure to read the full directions—acetaminophen overdose is particularly dangerous.

Baby painkillers, which are used to bring down a temperature, should start to take effect after half an hour.

Teething

While some babies seem to produce teeth with little apparent discomfort, others have a terrible time—and don't you know about it! The old wives' tale goes that the stronger the teeth, the more painful the teething. That may be little comfort when you are trying to soothe your moaning baby—and even less comforting to him.

Teething starts months before the first tooth appears, with dribbling, crying and chewing for relief. The first tooth should finally put in an appearance around six to eight months—or as late as a year old—and the last one should cut by two and a half. Take your baby to the dentist when you attend your own appointment. Let him sit on your lap while the dentist checks your teeth and then he can have a quick, gentle look in your baby's mouth, too. Keep on doing this and his first proper checkup will not be too alarming.

SIGNS OF TEETHING TROUBLES INCLUDE:

🐦 A baby who is fretful and clingy but has no other signs of illness.

🐦 Red, swollen gums.

🐦 Sometimes the edge of the tooth will be visible under the gum.

🐦 Your baby tries to chew his fingers and anything else he can put in his mouth.

WHAT YOU CAN DO:

🐦 Rub his gums with your clean little finger to relieve the pressure.

🐦 Cool his gums with chilled teething rings or cold carrot sticks (if he's advanced enough with his eating). Don't freeze the teething ring—these have been known to cause frostbite in babies! Just keep them in the refrigerator, rather than the freezer.

🐦 Homeopathic camomile (6c) or pulsatilla (6c) can be applied straight to the gums three or four times a day. You can also buy effective homeopathic teething granules to relieve the pain.

🐦 Avoid taking him out in a cold wind—it seems to make teething pain worse. If you must go out, keep his face warm with a hat and scarf.

🐦 Try not to use painkillers except under doctor's orders.

Seek help if your baby keeps refusing to eat or has other symptoms that don't seem to

COMMON ORDER OF TOOTH APPEARANCE

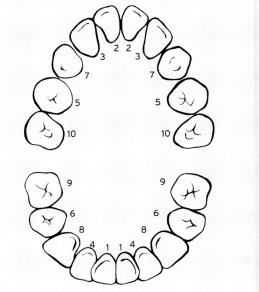

UPPER
10 5 7 3 2 2 3 7 5 10

LOWER
9 6 8 4 1 1 4 8 6 9

1 1st incisors
2 1st incisors
3 2nd incisors
4 2nd incisors
5 1st molars
6 1st molars
7 Eye
8 Eye
9 2nd molars
10 2nd molars

Your baby's instinct will be to bite on anything he can to soothe his aching gums.

...e linked to teething, and never blame anything more ...han fretfulness and dribbling on his teeth—it's a myth ...hat teething causes fever, diarrhea, vomiting, rashes, ...onvulsions, or loss of appetite.

The first teeth to come through are the lower front ...eeth, followed by the upper front teeth. Upper side teeth ...ome in next, followed by the lower side teeth.

Once your baby has several teeth, start good habits ...arly by turning tooth brushing into a game. Let him ...atch you brush your teeth first, and then offer him a ...aby toothbrush to play with (under strict and careful ...upervision). But to actually clean his teeth, use a piece of ...auze with a grain-sized piece of toothpaste on it to gently ...ub across his gums and the few teeth he has. The gums ...eed to be kept clean in order to keep the mouth free of the ...acteria that cause plaque.

...ething can cause great discomfort, and you will feel your baby's ...in and distress, too.

HEALTHY TEETH

🐦 Never give your baby a bottle or sippy cup containing sugary drinks or juice because his teeth will be constantly bathed in sugary fluid and this will encourage decay.

🐦 Don't give him sugary foods—these encourage a sweet tooth and exacerbate his risk of cavities.

🐦 Make sure his diet is rich in calcium and vitamin D, essential for the formation of healthy permanent teeth, which are already developing in the baby's jawbones. Dairy products and fish (especially herrings and sardines) are great foods for healthy teeth when your baby's old enough to eat them.

🐦 Discuss toothpaste with your pediatrician—she will know if you are in an area where the local water is high in fluoride, in which case you may want to avoid fluoride toothpastes. Although fluoride reduces the risk of dental decay, too much of it can cause a condition called fluorosis, which causes unattractive pitting and speckling of the dental enamel when the permanent teeth come through. If you are using a toothpaste with fluoride in it, use the tiniest amount—a little goes a long way!

Socializing Your Baby

alone. At four months he could hold his arms up in anticipation of you picking him up, and between five and six months he will have started using different expressions to greet different people. The people he knows and loves are greeted with smiles, while those who are strangers are given a recognizable expression of fear.

Seize on his interest in other people as an opportunity to help his social development. Introduce him to other babies via a mother and baby group, so he can get used to playing alongside other children prior to actually playing with them. This is also the time to get him used to other adults—he needs to be able to cope with babysitters and relatives looking after him. If you are going back to work,

Most children are naturally sociable—playing with baby friends is great entertainment for little ones.

The more sociable you are, the more likely it is that your baby will be sociable, too.

When your baby is around six months old, you may be aware that he has started pulling people's hair, or apparently slapping them on the face. It's not naughty behavior, but your baby's way of demonstrating the social skills he's already acquired in his short life.

He knows how to start a conversation with you by engaging your attention in some way, and he knows how to end the conversation by turning away or appearing bored.

From three months old he has disliked being deprived of social contact, and will show his feelings by crying if he's left

Taking your baby swimming helps with your child's physical and social development.

The childcare you choose can further help his social skills if your baby is placed in a daycare center or in a family daycare with a group of other children. A nanny-share is another good option if you don't want your baby to lead a solitary life.

BABY CLUBS

🐦 Check out your local swimming pool—find out if they run mother and baby swimming sessions, or classes.

🐦 Baby music lessons—a great chance to test their percussion skills and exercise their vocal cords with other children.

🐦 Baby gym—your baby can totter and tumble with other babies in a soft, safe environment.

CHOOSING CHILDCARE

🐦 **NANNY** Look for someone who instinctively warms to your baby, and vice versa. It sounds obvious, but she should also be fluent in your baby's mother tongue, as your baby will be relying on the nanny to gather much of his early vocabulary.

🐦 **FAMILY DAYCARE** is cheaper than a nanny and a good halfway house if you don't want to go the whole way and use a nursery. Choose someone who shares your philosophies on child rearing, and ask to visit the carer's home when the other children in her charge are around.

🐦 **DAYCARE CENTER** Check that it feels warm and welcoming, and that the children seem happy. It should also have an outdoor play area.

🐦 **AU PAIR** An au pair must have previous experience with children and be able to demonstrate this when she meets your baby. It's also crucial that you get on with her and that she fits into your family's way of doing things, as she will be living with you for several months.

🐦 **BABYSITTER** Many babysitters are students, so be confident that he or she is capable of looking after your child. Before you employ a babysitter for the first time, invite her over so you can meet her and see how she reacts to your baby. You may not be employing a babysitter very often, and may not even be able to use the same one regularly. Be sure that she will be able to cope with calming your baby if he wakes when you are out. In an ideal world you will find a babysitter who can come in for a few hours occasionally when your baby is awake (and you are napping or getting on with work)—that way, your baby will recognize her and won't be frightened if she's the one who picks him up when he cries on the evening that you're out.

Your Baby's First Year

Use these pages to record your baby's most memorable milestones.

Started to crawl (Where were you, how did it happen, who was with you?)

....

....

....

....

Cut the first tooth (Was it painful? Which tooth came first?)

....

....

....

....

First words

....

....

....

....

....

....

Favorite activity

Favorite book

Favorite game

Favorite song

Favorite food

Favorite toy

More Memorable Events

Use these pages to record more memorable events in your baby's life.

Started to walk

Started to run

Climbed out of his crib

First recognizable words

First day at playgroup or nursery

Baby's First Birthday!

Make sure your baby's birthday party is a relaxing and enjoyable occasion for you, too.

It's a whole year since your baby was born, and it can feel like a lifetime has passed. Your baby's first birthday is a day of celebration for you—but, if you are planning a party, and you want him to enjoy it, put his needs first.

🦢 Plan a short, sweet party for a time when he is going to be awake and happy—e.g. for one hour, mid-afternoon.

🦢 Invite just a few guests—and stick to people he knows and loves and who are important in his life. This could be one or two babies he meets regularly and likes. Choose your baby's friends rather than the babies of your friends. Invite the person who looks after him regularly—a loved babysitter or nanny, or the staff who look after him at his regular daycare center.

🦢 Stick to easy foods that he can enjoy—choose brightly colored vegetable sticks rather than brightly colored cakes,

Don't be surprised if your baby cries—too much fun may be overwhelming for the guest of honour.

candies, and cookies. It's a party, but not an excuse to blow the baby diet.

🦢 Choose music you know he enjoys—the calming classical music he's come to recognize is good for background when people arrive. A few nursery rhymes are great if you plan to play some games.

🦢 Keep gifts simply wrapped so that he can enjoy opening them. Don't be surprised if the wrapper is of more interest than the present inside!

🦢 Plan simple activies that he can join in, such as a nursery rhyme sing-along. It's best to stick to those he's already discovered at his baby music classes, or at his daycare. Anything new could be daunting and frightening, especially when there are so many people around and your baby is the focus of attention.

If she's not daunted by the occasion, your baby may just lap up all the attention she can get!

NOW YOUR BABY IS ONE!

Your baby is getting more adventurous all the time. As he moves into his second year, revisit your childproofing by getting down to his level and finding the danger zones that he'll make a beeline for. Over the next six months he will:

🐦 Become a more proficient walker, and by 18 months some babies can run.

🐦 Start babbling—it will appear that he's telling you something fascinating, but it won't be comprehensible for a while yet.

🐦 Be more skilled with his toys—learning to build a small tower of blocks. He'll also start stacking toys inside each other and will understand the idea of tidying up after playtime (make the most of it!).

🐦 Start scribbling pictures—keep pens and pencils out of his reach when he's unsupervised.

🐦 Develop a good memory for games.

🐦 Begin to use his imagination—rocking a baby doll, pushing a toy buggy with teddies in it, or using a pretend telephone.

PARTY SPREAD

Stick to simple foods that look good, choosing ingredients that adults can enjoy but that won't be out of bounds to the birthday girl or boy!

🐦 Sticks of carrot, bell peppers, cucumber, snowpeas, and green beans with avocado dip. (Mash an avocado in a food processor with lemon juice, cilantro, and cream cheese.)

🐦 Cold organic chipolata sausages.

🐦 Fruit salad kebabs—skewer seedless grapes with strawberries, pineapple chunks, and slices of banana. (Remove the fruit from the skewer for your baby and keep the skewer out of reach.)

🐦 Sandwiches—make small sandwiches (quarters or triangles, with the crusts removed) with fillings such as soft cream cheese, tuna, banana, chopped chicken, and cucumber.

🐦 Birthday cake—stick to a simple sponge with a buttercream filling, prettily decorated.

Be prepared to be silly—it's good practice for all the children's parties to follow!

One Today

Use these pages to record your baby's first birthday.

Who came?

The party invitation (stick baby's invite here)

What we did

You made us all laugh when...

Use the following spaces for photos to remember the day by.

Index